30 Days

TO A MORE POWERFUL VOCABULARY

30 Days

TO A MORE POWERFUL VOCABULARY

Dr. Wilfred Funk
&
Norman Lewis

G

GALLERY BOOKS

NEW YORK LONDON TORONTO SYDNEY NEW DELHI

Gallery Books
An Imprint of Simon & Schuster, Inc.
1230 Avenue of the Americas
New York, NY 10020

This Gallery Books trade paperback edition June 2022

GALLERY BOOKS and colophon are registered trademarks of
Simon & Schuster, Inc.

For information about special discounts for bulk purchases, please contact
Simon & Schuster Special Sales at 1-866-506-1949 or
business@simonandschuster.com.

The Simon & Schuster Speakers Bureau can bring authors
to your live event. For more information or to book an event,
contact the Simon & Schuster Speakers Bureau at 1-866-248-3049
or visit our website at www.simonspeakers.com.

Interior design by Kathryn Kenney-Peterson

1   3   5   7   9   10   8   6   4   2

ISBN 978-1-9821-9471-0

To Walter M. Garcia

Contents

Pronunciation Key

The phonetic transcription of most words in the following pages will be self-explanatory and completely clear and obvious. Only a very few symbols have to be practiced and understood before you start.

1. ə: *This is the phonetic symbol (called schwa) which indicates "a weak, neutral vowel sound occurring in most of the unstressed syllables in English speech, as the* a *in* alone, *the* e *in* happen, *the* u *in* circus."*

2. ō: *The vowel sound in* gō, nō, lōw, sō, *etc.*

3. o͞o: *The vowel sound in* fo͞ol, so͞on, no͞on, etc.

4. zh: *The sound of the* s *in* occasion, treasure, measure, leisure, *etc.*

5. o͝o: *The vowel sound of* bo͝ok, lo͝ok, *etc.*

Many words are stressed on more than one syllable, although only one syllable may receive the *primary* or strongest accent. When you say *pyromaniac,* for example, you place the strongest stress on the third syllable (*ma*)—that is, you say the third syllable with the greatest loudness. But the first syllable, *py,* also receives some stress; that is, you say it louder than *ro, i,* or *ac.* To show these distinctions, we will capitalize and accent the strongest syllable (MAY´), and only accent the second strongest (py´). *Pyromaniac* is thus phonetically rewritten as py´-ro-MAY´-nee-ak. Further examples:

satiated: SAY´-shee-ay´-təd

archaeology: ahr´-kee-OL´-ə-jee

opinionated: ə-PIN´-yə-nay´-təd

braggadocio: brag´-ə-DŌ´-shee-ō

---

* *Funk & Wagnalls Standard College Dictionary* (New York: Funk & Wagnalls, 1968).

X	2	3	4	5	6	7
8	9	10	11	12	13	14
15	16	17	18	19	20	21
22	23	24	25	26	27	28
29	30					

Give Us Fifteen
Minutes a Day

Your boss has a bigger vocabulary than you have.

That's one good reason why he's your boss.

This discovery has been made in the word laboratories of the world. Not by theoretical English professors, but by practical, hard-headed scientists who have been searching for the secrets of success.

After a host of experiments and years of testing they have found out:

That if your vocabulary is limited, your chances of success are
limited.

That one of the easiest and quickest ways to get ahead is by
consciously building up your knowledge of words.

That the vocabulary of the average person almost stops
growing by the middle twenties.

And that from then on it is necessary to have an intelligent
plan if progress is to be made. No hit-or-miss methods
will do.

It has long since been satisfactorily established that a high executive does not have a large vocabulary merely because of the opportunities of his position. That would be putting the cart before the horse. Quite the reverse is true. His skill in words was a tremendous help in getting him his job.

Dr. Johnson O'Connor of the Human Engineering Laboratory of Boston and of the Stevens Institute of Technology in Hoboken, New Jersey, gave a vocabulary test to one hundred young men who were studying to be industrial executives.

Five years later, *all*, without exception, of those who had passed in the upper 10 percent had executive positions, while *not a single young man of the lower 25 percent had become an executive.*

Some of the factors that lead to success can be measured as scientifically as the contents of a test tube, and it has been discovered that the one and only common characteristic of outstandingly successful people is "an extensive knowledge of the exact meaning of English words."

Vocabulary is one indication of intelligence. Learning power measurably sharpens when vocabulary increases. Here's the proof.

Two classes in a high school were selected for an experiment. The ages and background of the members of both groups were the same, and each group represented a similar cross-section of the community. One, the control class, took the normal courses. The other class had, in addition, special and rigorous vocabulary training. At the end of the period the grades of the students in the vocabulary class surpassed the grades of the members of the control group, not only in English, but in every other subject, including mathematics and the sciences.

Similarly, Professor Lewis M. Terman of Stanford University found that a vocabulary test is as accurate a measure of intelligence as any three units of the standard and accepted Stanford-Binet I.Q. tests.

Words are the tools of thinking. It naturally follows, then, that the more words you have at your command, the clearer and more accurate your thinking will be.

Words are your medium of exchange, the coin with which you do business with all those around you. With words you relate to people, communicate your feelings and thoughts to them, influence them, persuade them. In short, through words you shape your own destiny. For your words are your personality; your vocabulary is you.

Words are explosive. Phrases are packed with TNT. A single word can destroy a friendship, can start or end a marital battle, can land a large order. The right phrases in the mouths of clerks have quadrupled the sales of a department store. The wrong words used by a campaign orator have lost an election. Four unfortunate words—"Rum, Romanism, and Rebellion"—used in a Republican campaign speech threw the Catholic vote and the presidential victory to Grover Cleveland.

Armies fight for phrases: "Make the world safe for Democracy"; "V for Victory"; "Remember Pearl Harbor."

Words have changed the direction of history. Words can also change the direction of your life. They can raise a person from mediocrity to success.

We submit that if you methodically increase your vocabulary you will improve your chances for success.

This book enlists active cooperation, continuous written and oral response. It will test you every step of the way, it will demand unceasing feedback from you, and thus it will make words your friends and allies.

We expect to prove to you that developing a rich and robust vocabulary can be both fun and challenging.

Give us fifteen minutes a day, and we will guarantee that at the end of a month, when you have turned over the last page of this book, your words, your reading, your conversation, and your life will all have a new and deeper meaning for you.

For words can make you great!

✗	✗	3	4	5	6	7
8	9	10	11	12	13	14
15	16	17	18	19	20	21
22	23	24	25	26	27	28
29	30					

Take This Twelve-Minute Test of Your Verbal Power

First, we will take your word portrait.

When the picture is finished, you will know how you look to others as a conversationalist and how you may appear when you write a simple social note or a business letter.

The lines of your likeness that are to be drawn here will indicate the extent of your vocabulary, the facility with which you can recall and use words, and the knowledge that you have of their precise meanings. There will also be brief spelling and pronunciation tests so that we can get a complete picture.

You will find the tests in this chapter simple and entertaining. They will take exactly twelve minutes, and when you are through and have checked your score, you will know what's wrong, if anything, with your vocabulary and your use of words. You will, in short, have painted your own word portrait. Then, in the chapters that follow, we will show you how to strengthen any weak points that may have appeared.

How do words treat you? Are you comfortable with them? Do they come easily to you? When you write and speak, do your words paint the sort of picture of you that will do you the most good in this highly competitive world? Does your language usually present a true reflection of your mind, your emotions, and your personality? Or does it sometimes betray you and blur your thoughts? Do people occasionally misunderstand you? Or can you compel them to listen, react, obey?

Like everyone else, you want certain things from life. No matter what those benefits are, or what particular way you have chosen to go about getting them, you know that your first and most effective means will be the words you use.

In short, the satisfaction and the success you get out of life depend very greatly on the skill with which you communicate your needs, your desires, your opinions, to others.

Ready to discover what your command of language says about you?

TEST I
VERBAL SPEED (ELEMENTARY)

DIRECTIONS: Write in the blank space next to each of the words in the following list another word *that begins with S* and has a meaning directly *opposite* to the given word.

Time: 60 seconds

EXAMPLE: *fast*   *slow*

             sweet *sour*

             buy   *sell*

START TIMING:

1. tall   S _short_
2. north   S _outh_
3. happy   S _ad_
4. different   S _ame_
5. dangerous   S _afe_
6. big   S _mall_
7. dull   S _____
8. noisy   S _till_
9. sit   S _tand_
10. receive   S _end_

End Timing

(Answers for these tests will be found at the end of the chapter.)
You have just been tested for fluency.

You should have breezed through this test at high speed in less than sixty seconds with no hesitancy and no mistakes. If you had to think for more than an instant to recall the proper word, it is likely that you experience some difficulty in expressing your thoughts. You are probably seeing people who are not as bright as you getting ahead of you. You may often wonder: "What have they got that I haven't got?"

Your lack of an adequate word arsenal may have seriously handicapped you. If so, this book is designed for you. It will give you the chance to go to work and overcome your obstacle.

TEST II
VERBAL SPEED (ADVANCED)

DIRECTIONS: As in the previous test, write a word beginning with S which is *opposite* in meaning to each of the following.

Time: 90 seconds

START TIMING:

1. generous   S _stingy_
2. meaningless   S _significant_
3. believing   S _suspicious_
4. complicated   S _simple_
5. doubtful   S _sure_
6. careful   S _sloppy_
7. wakefulness   S _sleepiness_
8. rough   S _smooth_
9. objective   S _subjective_
10. laugh   S _nawl_

End Timing

Speed and accuracy are again of great importance. If you completed this test in ninety seconds and got eight out of ten correct, you are far above the average and you doubtless show unusual skill and ease in translating your thoughts into the proper words; you are going to make swift progress in the lessons that are ahead.

If, on the other hand, you exceeded your time limit, or if you were wrong in five or more words, it is critically necessary that you start today to improve your vocabulary. We are dealing in this book with one of the richest languages in the world, and with a little practice and patience you can easily make its great wealth your own.

TEST III
SYNONYM RECALL

Here is a test of your skill from another point of view. You have been working with *antonyms*, or words of opposite meanings. How will you do with *synonyms*, or words of the same, or almost the same, meanings? It is highly important that you have a wealth of synonyms, which are analogous to the many colors on an artist's palette, at your command. Synonyms within easy reach help you paint for your listener the many shades of your thoughts; they lend variety and interest to your conversation and writing.

DIRECTIONS: In the spaces given below write two words that are synonymous with the given word.

Time: 2 minutes

EXAMPLE: beautiful   lovely, pretty

strong   rugged, powerful

short   brief, concise

This test should be finished within the time limit, as there are many more than two synonyms for each of these words. Check with a dictionary if your answers are not found in the list at the end of the chapter.

START TIMING:

1. defects (*noun*)   _____   _____
2. desires (*noun*)   _____   _____
3. true   _____   _____
4. suitable   _____   _____
5. luminous   _____   _____
6. loathing (*noun*)   _____   _____
7. doubtful   _____   _____
8. vulgar   _____   _____
9. admiration   _____   _____
10. very   _____   _____

End Timing

TEST IV
SYNONYM RECOGNITION

We have tested your ability to recall the synonyms for a given word. We are now going to test your ability to *recognize* synonyms when you see them.

DIRECTIONS: In the following list there are sixteen words. Start with *infidel* and put a small figure 1 above it. Run through the list until you find another word that has the same or similar meaning. Put a 1 above that one. Then try the second word on the list, *large*, putting a figure 2 above it, and search for a word of similar meaning and mark it 2. And so on until you have eight pairs of synonyms or words of similar meaning.

Time: 90 seconds

START TIMING:

infidel	ingenious	occur	aberration
large	happen	persuade	kidnap
bulky	eccentricity	clever	unbeliever
abduct	unsophisticated	induce	ingenuous

End Timing

TEST V
HOMONYMS

DIRECTIONS: Homonyms are words that are pronounced almost exactly alike but that differ considerably in meaning. Check the homonym that makes sense in each of the following sentences.

Time: 90 seconds

START TIMING:

1. Why does modern music have such a strange [(a) *affect*, (b) *effect*] on you?

2. Most buildings have [(a) *stationery*, (b) *stationary*] walls.

3. The [(a) *principal*, (b) *principle*] features of Southern California are sunshine and smog.

4. Sitting contentedly by the fire, the cat licked [(a) *it's*, (b) *its*] paws.

5. His vocal [(a) *cords*, (b) *chords*] are inflamed.

6. He sat for hours [(a) *poring*, (b) *pouring*] over the dictionary.

7. He listened with [(a) *baited*, (b) *bated*] breath for the second shoe to fall.

8. Admiral Nelson is famous for one of the most important [(a) *navel*, (b) *naval*] encounters in British history.

9. The scene of the accident was lighted by a huge [(a) *flare*, (b) *flair*].

10. The boxer made a [(a) *feint*, (b) *faint*] with his left.

End Timing

TEST VI
UNDERSTANDING WORDS

DIRECTIONS: Check the definition that properly explains the italicized word in each phrase.

Time: 2 minutes

START TIMING:

1. An *acrimonious* argument
   (a) long-winded
   (b) sharp, biting, sarcastic
   (c) dull, pointless, and incoherent

2. A *soporific* lecture
   (a) so boring as to put one to sleep
   (b) brilliant and informative
   (c) well-attended

3. *Panacea* for social ills
   (a) direct cause
   (b) cure-all
   (c) condition encouraging continuation

4. An *evanescent* feeling
   (a) fading away quickly
   (b) composed of both dread and desire
   (c) so unique that it is experienced by very few people

5. Overwhelmed by *ennui*
   (a) fear
   (b) dissatisfaction and boredom resulting from inactivity
   (c) a sudden awareness of one's unconscious motivation

6. A *facetious* remark
   (a) witty or joking at an inappropriate time
   (b) tending to make peace between people in conflict
   (c) totally irrelevant to the situation

7. A *maelstrom* of emotions
   - (a) complete lack
   - (b) catalogue in chronological order
   - (c) violent, stormy confusion
8. *Maudlin* attitudes
   - (a) self-destructive
   - (b) tearfully and excessively sentimental
   - (c) showing great maturity at a surprisingly early age
9. Drove *adroitly*
   - (a) skillfully
   - (b) nervously
   - (c) inattentively
10. A *sardonic* smile
    - (a) empty, meaningless
    - (b) open and trusting
    - (c) bitter and scornful

End Timing

TEST VII
SPELLING WITHOUT ERROR

Here are ten common words frequently misspelled by those whose linguistic ability needs sharpening. Check the form that looks right to you.

Time: 60 seconds

START TIMING:

1. (a) occurrance, (b) occurrence, (c) occurance
2. (a) ecstasy, (b) ecstacy, (c) extacy
3. (a) drunkeness, (b) drunkenness, (c) drunkedness
4. (a) embarassing, (b) embarrassing, (c) embarrasing
5. (a) irresistible, (b) irresistable, (c) irrisistible
6. (a) supersede, (b) supercede, (c) superceed
7. (a) disappoint, (b) dissapoint, (c) dissappoint
8. (a) occassional, (b) occasional, (c) ocassional
9. (a) indispensable, (b) indispensible, (c) indespensible
10. (a) perseverance, (b) perseverence, (c) perserverance

End Timing

TEST VIII
PRONOUNCING IN
THE EDUCATED MANNER

The pronunciation of American English is, admittedly, unstable: The sound of words changes according to geographical area, ethnic background, economic and social levels, etc. *Mary, marry,* and *merry,* for example, are pronounced almost identically in the Midwest and along much of the Pacific coastal regions; whereas in the East and South they sound very different. The first syllable of *orange* is pronounced *or* in California and *are* in New York. The vowel sound of *talk* and *walk* is uttered one way by a native of Brooklyn and quite another way by someone born in Los Angeles. Words like *either, tomato, tune, adult, licorice, strength,* and many others can often show the age, income, background, and sophistication of the speaker.

Nevertheless, one kind of pronunciation test will be useful in completing your verbal portrait. The following ten words, among many others, have both an illiterate or dialectal and an educated pronunciation. Say each one carefully according to its phonetic respelling, then check the form that sounds most nearly like what you ordinarily use in conversation.

The symbol ə is the sound of the *a* in *about* or in *Linda.*

Time: 90 seconds

START TIMING:

1. genuine   (a) JEN´yə-win
               (b) JEN´yə-wyne

2. athlete   (a) ATH´ə-leet
               (b) ATH´-leet

3. film   (a) FILM
               (b) FIL´-əm

4. modern   (a) MAHR´-dən
               (b) MOD´-ərn
               (c) MOD´-ərn

5. accept   (a) ək-SEPT´
               (b) ə-SEPT´

6. drowned (a) DROWN´dəd
               (b) DROWND

7. wrestle   (a) RESS´-əl
               (b) RASS´-əl

8. pattern   (a) PAT´-rən
               (b) PAT´-ərn

9. figure   (a) FIG´-yər
               (b) FIG´-ər

10. attacked (a) ə-TAK´-təd
               (b) ə-TAKT´

End Timing

Now you may relax. Your test of verbal power is concluded; your word portrait is finished. What you will see on the canvas—pleasant or unpleasant, encouraging or discouraging—is what the world sees when you write or speak. At this point, before you check your score, we offer you one important thought: No matter how good or bad your word power is today, it can be immeasurably better, more useful, more potent, in just thirty days.

SCORING

Determine your score for each test by comparing your answers with those given below:

TEST I:

    (1) short; (2) south; (3) sad; (4) same, similar; (5) safe;

    (6) small; (7) smart, sharp, sparkling, shiny; (8) silent, still;

    (9) stand; (10) send

Scoring: 2 points for each correct answer

Maximum score: 20 points

Your Score: _____

TEST II:

    (1) selfish, stingy; (2) sensible, significant; (3) skeptical,

suspicious; (4) simple; (5) sure; (6) slipshod, slovenly, sloppy;

    (7) sleep, sleepiness, slumber, somnolence; (8) smooth;

    (9) subjective; (10) sob, scowl

Scoring: 2 points for each correct answer

Maximum score: 20 points

Your Score: _____

TEST III:

    (1) shortcomings, imperfections, faults, weaknesses, deficiencies, blemishes

    (2) wishes, wants, longings, cravings, appetites

    (3) right, correct, truthful, genuine, straight, honest, faithful, veracious, pure

    (4) appropriate, consistent, fitting, fit, applicable

    (5) bright, lustrous, radiant, brilliant, vivid, gleaming, shining, glowing, lucid

    (6) disgust, aversion, detestation, antipathy, repugnance, abhorrence

    (7) ambiguous, vague, obscure, indefinite, loose, uncertain, dubious, questionable, dubitable

(8) rude, common, coarse, gross, ill-bred, low, obscene, ill-mannered, crass

(9) praise, approval, commendation, esteem, veneration, approbation

(10) extremely, exceedingly, highly, enormously, immensely, abundantly, terribly, quite

Scoring: 2 points for each question answered correctly
Failure to give 2 synonyms counts zero
Maximum score: 20 points

Your Score: _____

TEST IV:

(1) infidel	(1) unbeliever
(2) ingenious	(2) clever
(3) occur	(3) happen
(4) aberration	(4) eccentricity
(5) large	(5) bulky
(6) persuade	(6) induce
(7) kidnap	(7) abduct
(8) unsophisticated	(8) ingenuous

Scoring: 2 points for each correct pair
Maximum score: 16 points

Your Score: _____

TEST V:

(1) b; (2) b; (3) a; (4) b; (5) a; (6) a; (7) b; (8) b; (9) a; (10) a
Scoring: 1 point for each correct choice
Maximum score: 10 points

Your Score: _____

TEST VI:

(1) b; (2) a; (3) b; (4) a; (5) b; (6) a; (7) c; (8) b; (9) a; (10) c
Scoring: 2 points for each correct choice
Maximum score: 20 points

Your Score: _____

TEST VII:

(1) b; (2) a; (3) b; (4) b; (5) a; (6) a; (7) a; (8) b; (9) a; (10) a

Scoring: 2 points for each correct choice

Maximum score: 20 points

Your Score: _____

TEST VIII:

(1) a; (2) b; (3) a; (4) c; (5) a; (6) b; (7) a; (8) b; (9) a; (10) b

Scoring: 2 points for each correct choice

Maximum score: 20 points

Your Score: _____

Now add your scores in the 8 tests to arrive at your total score out of a maximum of 146.

Your Total Score: _____

INTERPRETATION

YOUR TOTAL SCORE:

120–146   You belong in the top 10 percent of the literate popula-
            tion of this country and you should be on the way to a
            high position in your vocational, intellectual, and social
            life. You will get a special pleasure out of this book as you
            perfect a vocabulary that is already sound.

99–119   Your vocabulary is about average and is therefore not
            helping you gain success as fast as you might otherwise
            be able to. Start building your vocabulary today and
            make this interesting work a daily habit. The new words
            you learn will acquaint you with new fields of knowledge,
            and there will be many additional subtle and indirect re-
            wards. Remember: There is no easier way to achieve suc-
            cess than by adding to your vocabulary.

98 and below This score shows a definitely impoverished vocabulary;
            your weakness in words may be holding you back. It would
            be a foolish and fatal mistake not to do something imme-
            diately about it. Here are two don'ts for you: Don't let your
            low score unduly disturb you. And don't feel that only a
            university graduate can be an expert user of words. Shake-
            speare attended school for ten years all told. Robert Burns,
            the Scottish poet, was a day laborer without education.
            Neither Charles Lamb nor Charles Dickens had enough
            formal schooling to talk about. And Abraham Lincoln
            didn't know what the inside of a school looked like. They
            and many others like them became masters of speech.
            They achieved their effectiveness by industry and practice.
            So can you. And when you do, your reward will be great.

The beauty of this book is that you start to benefit—not after months
of trial—but from the first day and with the first chapter.

X	X	X	4	5	6	7
8	9	10	11	12	13	14
15	16	17	18	19	20	21
22	23	24	25	26	27	28
29	30					

The Romance of Words

From now on we want you to look at words intently, to be inordinately curious about them, and to examine them syllable by syllable, letter by letter. They are your tools of understanding and self-expression. Collect them. Keep them in condition. Learn how to handle them. Develop a fastidious, but not a fussy, choice. Work always toward good taste in their use. Train your ear for their harmonies.

We urge you not to take words for granted just because they have been part of your daily speech since childhood. You must examine them. Turn them over and over as though you were handling a coin, and see the seal and superscription on each one. *We would like you actually to fall in love with words.*

Words are not dead things. They are fairly wriggling with life. They are the exciting and mysterious tokens of our thoughts, and like human beings, they are born, come to maturity, grow old, and die, and some-times they are even reborn in a new age. A word, from its birth to its death, is a process, not a static thing.

Words, like living trees, have roots, branches, and leaves.

Shall we stay with this analogy for a few moments, and see how perfect it is?

The story of the root of a word is the story of its origin. The study of origins is called *etymology,* which in turn has *its* roots in the Greek word *etymon,* meaning "true or original meaning," and the Greek ending *-logia,* meaning "science or study." So *etymology* means the science or study of true or original meanings.

Every word in our language is a frozen metaphor, a frozen picture. It is this poetry behind words that gives language its overwhelming power. And the more intimately we know the romance that lies within each word, the better understanding we will have of its meaning.

For instance, on certain occasions you will probably say that you have "calculated" the cost of something or other. What does the term *calculate* really mean? Here is the story. Years ago, ancient Romans had an instrument called a *hodometer,* or "road measurer," which corresponded to our modern taxi meter. If you had hired a two-wheeled Roman vehicle to ride, say, to the Forum, you might have found in the back a tin can with a revolving cover that held a quantity of pebbles. This can was so contrived that each time the wheel turned, the metal cover also revolved, and a pebble dropped through a hole into the receptacle below. At the end of your trip you counted the pebbles and *calculated* your bill. You see, the Latin word for pebble was *calculus,* and that's where our word "calculate" comes from.

There are, of course, many words with much simpler histories than this. When you speak of a *surplus,* for instance, you are merely saying that you have a *sur* (French for "over") *plus* (French for "more") or a *surplus.* That is, you have an "over-more" than you need.

Should you be in a snooty mood for the nonce, and happen to look at someone rather haughtily, your friends might call you *supercilious,* a word that comes from the Latin *supercilium,* meaning that "eyebrow" you just raised. That person you are so fond of, who has become your *companion,* is simply one who eats bread with you—from Latin *cum,* "with," and *panis*, "bread." *Trumps* in bridge is from the French *triomphe* or "triumph," an old-time game of cards. In modern cards, one suit is allowed to triumph over, or to "trump," the other suits. And still again, in the army, the *lieutenant* is literally one who takes the place of the captain when the latter is not around—from the French *lieu* (we use it in "in lieu of") and *tenir*, "to hold." The *captain*, in turn, derives from the Latin word *caput* ("head"). *Colonel* comes from *columna* (the "column" that he leads).

If, by any chance, you would like to tease your friend the Wall Street *broker*, just tell him that his professional title came from the Middle English word *brocour*, a "broacher," or one who opens, or broaches, a cask to draw off the wine or liquor. We still employ the same word in the original sense when we say "He broached [or opened up] the subject." The broacher, or broker, became in time a salesman of wine, then of other things, such as stocks and bonds.

These are the roots of words. We next come to the branches. The branches of our language tree are those many groups of words that have grown out from one original root.

Let's take an example. From the Latin root *spectare*, which means "to look," more than 240 English words have sprouted. We find the root in such words as *spectacle* (those things you look through), *spectator* (one who looks or watches), *respect* (the tribute you give to a person you care to look at again), and *inspect* (to look into). When you treat someone with *disrespect*, you make it plain that you do not care to look at him again (*dis*, "not"—*re*, "again"—*spect*, "look"). *Introspection* is a looking within.

Turning to the Greek language, which has so largely enriched our own, we discover *graphein*, "to write," another prolific source of English words. We have *telegraph* (writing from a distance), *phonograph* (writing by sound), *photograph* (writing by means of light), *stenographer* (one who does condensed writing), and *mimeograph* (to write a copy or imitation).

We have in our language a host of roots such as these. There is the Latin *spirare,* meaning "to blow or breathe," from which we get such English words as *inspire* (breathe into), *expire* (breathe out), *perspire* (breathe through), *respiration* (breathing again or often).

Our word "liable" comes from the Latin *ligare,* "to bind." This fascinating root has branched out into *oblige* and *obligate* (to bind to do something), *ligature* (bandage or binding), *ligament* (something that ties two things together), and, with the root no longer so obvious, *league* (those nations or other organizations that are bound together), and even the word *ally* (to bind to one another), which is from *ad* and *ligare.*

These, then, are the branches. We turn now to the leaves. If the roots are the origins of words and the branches are the word families that stem out of them, the leaves of this language tree would be the words themselves and their meanings.

Each given word, in its beginning, had, no doubt, only one meaning. But words are so full of life that they are continually sprouting the green shoots of new meanings.

Shall we choose just one word as an instance of the amazing vitality of language? The simple three-letter word *run,* up to this moment of writing, has more than ninety dictionary definitions. There are the *run* in your stocking, the *run* on the bank, and a *run* in baseball. The clock may *run* down, but you *run* up a bill. Colors *run.* You may *run* a race or *run* a business. You may have the *run* of the mill, or, quite different, the *run* of the house when you get the *run* of things. And this dynamic little word, we can assure you, has just begun its varied career with these examples.

Is it any wonder that our unabridged dictionaries contain hundreds of thousands of living and usable words, words sparkling with life, prolific in their breeding, luxuriant in their growth, continually shifting and changing in their meanings?

Words even have definite personalities and characters. They can be sweet, sour, discordant, musical. They can be sugary or acrid, soft or sharp, hostile or friendly.

From this time on, as we enter our word studies, try to become keenly aware of words. Look at them, if possible, with the fresh eyes of one who is seeing them for the first time. If we have persuaded you to do this, you will then be on the way to the success that can be won with a more powerful vocabulary.

X	X	X	X	5	6	7
8	9	10	11	12	13	14
15	16	17	18	19	20	21
22	23	24	25	26	27	28
29	30					

Words for Mature Minds

I

There are words in English that can be understood only by those who have lived and become mature. No explanation, no definitions, could make them clear to a child.

Here are ten such words. Pronounce each one aloud several times, following carefully the phonetic respelling. (Recall that the symbol ə has the sound of the *a* in *about* or in *Linda*.)

1. *vicarious* (vy-KAIR´-ee-əs)
2. *rationalize* (RASH´-ən-ə-lize)
3. *gregarious* (grə-GAIR´-ee-əs)
4. *obsequious* (əb-SEE´-kwee-əs)
5. *maudlin* (MAWD´-lin)
6. *ascetic* (a-SET´-ik)
7. *pander* (PAN´-dər)
8. *sublimate* (SUB´-lə-mate)
9. *wanton* (WAHN´-tən)
10. *effete* (ə-FEET´)

II

You might find it hard, perhaps absolutely impossible, to explain these terms to a nine-year-old boy or girl.

But you, an adult, will be able to comprehend them and to make them your property.

Let us discuss them, one by one. Here and there we will give you the etymology of the word, if its history is interesting and happens to throw any light on its present-day meaning.

1. *Vicarious.* This is an abstract word, but it is one that is easy for the grown-up mind to grasp. For example, there are two ways to travel: one by buying a steamship ticket and going to your destination, say Paris; the other by reading travel stories or travel circulars *about* Paris. In the first instance you have enjoyed your travel experience *directly.* In the second instance you have enjoyed it *vicariously.*

A child is learning about life when he "pretends," when he plays "store," or "house," or "doctor." Of course he is fully living the life that children do, but he is also living adult life, not directly, but *vicariously.* And owing to his emotional immaturity, he is not ready, at his age, to grasp the difference, in thought and effect, between actual living and *vicarious* living. When he is older and more mature he will live less *vicariously* and more actually, and then he will be able to appreciate the significance of the word.

You, as an older person, will recognize that you are escaping from the real world and are living for the moment a *vicarious* existence and are having *vicarious* joys and sorrows when you are reading a book. You are living, not your own life, but the lives of the characters of the story. The lonely, friendless woman living a life of suffocating routine or hopeless boredom can sit glued, hour after hour, to the television set. She then becomes the heroine in a passionate love story; she can experience *vicariously* all the excitement, romance, thrills, and exotic adventure that her real life is empty of. She can be a spy, a murderer, a figure of international intrigue, a visitor from another planet. She has only to twist the dial and change her drab existence into an abundant, fulfilling, and electric (but *vicarious*) reality.

2. *Rationalize.* You, as a human being, tend to *rationalize.* So do all of us. There are selfish men, for instance, who will never give anything to charity. They don't wish to regard themselves as selfish, however. They prefer to think that charity is harmful to the poor and demoralizes those who receive it. In this way the miser can save his money and his face at the same time. He is *rationalizing* his selfish act and the *rationalization* makes him feel better.

In similar fashion, a father who is angry may spank his boy merely to relieve his own personal feelings. But in self-defense he will *rationalize* his action by making himself believe that the spanking has been done for the good of the child.

The term *rationalize* has a number of meanings, but the most common one refers to the unconscious process of thought by which one justifies a discreditable act, and by which one offers to oneself and the world a better motive for one's action than the true motive.

3. *Gregarious.* This term comes from the Latin word *grex,* "a flock," as of sheep, and you know sheep like to stay together. If you are a *gregarious* type, you are a friendly person, a good mixer; you like to be with other people. That is, you are the extremely sociable kind. Because you are *gregarious*, you enjoy parties, crowded theaters, and dance floors; you like to be where folks flock in small or large numbers. Because people are *gregarious*, they get married, have families, live in thronging cities, sing and play together. A hunger for love or friendship and a feeling of kinship with other human beings are normal and common human traits. It is the herd instinct that makes people, to a greater or lesser degree, *gregarious.*

4. *Obsequious.* The beggar, the underling, the lackey, and the flunkey all tend to be *obsequious.* Those who wait on others in an inferior capacity and whose lives and jobs depend on the whims of their masters

are apt to be cringing and fawning. They are often excessively, sickeningly, and insincerely polite. If your waiter in a restaurant believes that you are the type who will tip him well, watch how *obsequious* he will be, how he will bow to you and attend to your slightest wish. If you don't leave the expected tip, however, his *obsequiousness* will quickly vanish and he will not (*ob*, "upon," *sequor*, "follow") follow submissively upon your wishes.

5. *Maudlin.* A *maudlin* person is one who is supersentimental and gushing, who cries easily and without much cause. People who are *maudlin* in their affections usually overdo the act, and their love becomes tiresome and offensive. The word *maudlin* can also be applied to those who have been made foolish and silly by too much drinking.

Here, incidentally, is an odd word history. Mary Magdalene, who washed the feet of Christ, has often been pictured with her eyes red from weeping. In time, the name Magdalene was contracted into the adjective *maudlin*.

6. *Ascetic.* The *ascetic* is one who is given to severe self-denial and austerity, one who practices rigid abstinence, often for religious reasons. When you say that a man is an *ascetic*, you mean that he is one who shuns all the luxuries and physical pleasures of life. Anyone who eats and drinks heartily or who otherwise dissipates is the precise opposite of an *ascetic*, and does not believe in *asceticism* (a-SET´-ə-siz-əm).

7. *Pander.* This verb literally means to minister to the gratification of the passions and prejudices of others, usually to one's own profit. Novels that give blow-by-blow descriptions of bedroom intimacies, and motion pictures and TV shows that omit none of the gory details of violence, torture, and murder, have been accused of *pandering* to the so-called base instincts and morbid curiosity of their readers and audience. Ruthless dictators of the past are said to have *pandered* to the lowest instincts of the mobs, to selfishness, cruelty, and greed, in order to gain power. *Pander*, therefore, is an unpleasant word with an unpleasant meaning. The noun *panderer* has a still more restricted meaning and frequently

signifies a man who procures women for others, just as Pandarus, the leader of the Lycians in the Trojan War, is said to have procured the lovely lady Cressida for Troilus.

8. *Sublimate.* This word originally came from the Latin *sublimatus,* "raised on high," and is closely related to "sublime." When the energies of a potential hoodlum or gangster are channeled into athletic games, into a business career, or into some other useful endeavor, his former destructive activities are said to have been *sublimated.* Psychologists tell us that unfulfilled sexual needs are often *sublimated* into creative activities in art or poetry, that the surgeon or butcher may be a *sublimated* sadist, that the psychopathic exhibitionist becomes an actor. To *sublimate,* then, is to express primitive and socially unacceptable drives in constructive ways, usually through completely unconscious processes. A female whose unconscious desire it is to enslave men, to dominate and destroy all males, becomes the energetic and successful business executive or the president of a college with a largely male faculty, and only her psychiatrist knows that she is *sublimating.*

9. *Wanton.* Call a woman *wanton* and you are saying that she indulges every passion, that she is lewd and lascivious—in short, that she believes in living it up, with no thought of consequences or of the morrow's hangover. She never expects to be sorry in the morning, and she never is.

10. *Effete.* When animals, plants, or soil are worn out and incapable of producing, they are called *effete* (Latin *ex,* "out," *fetus,* "having produced"). More commonly, though, this adjective is applied to humans or their institutions, and when you refer to ancient Rome at the time of its fall as an *effete* civilization, you mean that it was degenerate, worn out, sterile, devoid of vigor, weakened by luxury, self-indulgence, and soft living.

III

Now we want to help you make these ten words your own possessions, your private property. Below are the definitions of the ten terms we are studying in this chapter. Take your pencil and write each word next to its definition.

1. M _____ tearfully or excessively sentimental

2. P _____ to cater to base desires

3. G _____ preferring the company of others to solitude

4. E _____ spent; exhausted; barren of energy; worn out by rich or effortless existence

5. A _____ practicing extreme self-denial

6. V _____ enjoyed by one person through his sympathetic but indirect participation in the experience of another (real or fictional) person; substitutional

7. R _____ to attribute one's actions to rational and creditable motives, without an adequate analysis of the true and usually unconscious motives

8. O _____ servilely attentive; fawning

9. S _____ to direct energy from its primitive and destructive aim to one that is culturally or ethically higher and therefore socially acceptable

10. W _____ unchaste; lewd; licentious; marked by arrogant recklessness of justice, of the feelings of others, or the like; also, having no just provocation; willfully malicious

ANSWERS: (1) maudlin; (2) pander; (3) gregarious; (4) effete; (5) ascetic; (6) vicarious; (7) rationalize; (8) obsequious; (9) sublimate; (10) wanton

IV

Keep your pencil always ready. This is a workbook, a self-teaching manual, and we want you to write in it continually. The only way you can feel at home with new words is by saying them, writing them, using them.

Now take the following eight words and change them into other parts of speech according to the instructions. Be sure in each case that the resulting sentence or phrase makes sense.

1. Change *vicarious* to an adverb, as in *He traveled*
   _____.

2. Change *rationalize* to a noun, as in *You are guilty of*
   _____.

3. Change *gregarious* to a noun, as in *No one doubts the*
   _____ *of human beings.*

4. Change *obsequious* to an adverb, as in *He obeyed*
   _____.

5. Change *ascetic* to a noun referring to the philosophy or practice, as in *He is a believer in* _____.

6. Change *pander* to a noun, as in *He is a* _____ *to the greed of others.*

7. Change *sublimate* to an adjective, as in *His* _____ *passion gives power to his poetry.*

8. Change *wanton* to a noun, as in *Hers was a life characterized by* _____.

ANSWERS: (1) vicariously; (2) rationalization; (3) gregariousness; (4) obsequiously; (5) asceticism; (6) panderer; (7) sublimated; (8) wantonness

V

From your work so far with these ten words, you should now have a fairly good idea of how they may be used in sentences, even if you may have met some of them for the first time. Test yourself. Without referring to the list on the previous page, try to fill in the required word in the sentences that follow. Note that any one of the several forms of each word may be needed. Use your pencil: The mere physical act of writing a word will help to fix it in your mind.

1. Marie is too _____ to be happy without friends.

2. The waiter bowed _____ to every wealthy customer who came in the restaurant.

3. His dissipated life has sapped his ambition and health and made him _____.

4. The motion picture was so sickeningly _____ that most of the audience left in disgust.

5. Mothers feel a _____ pleasure in their children's accomplishments.

6. Be honest with yourself. Don't try to _____ what you are doing.

7. He lived the life of an _____, for he abhorred self-indulgence and luxury.

8. The dishonest politician _____ to the greed and thoughtlessness of the mob.

9. Some say that all great art is a _____ of primitive instincts.

10. She led a fruitless, _____, uncontrolled life.

ANSWERS: (1) gregarious; (2) obsequiously; (3) effete; (4) maudlin; (5) vicarious; (6) rationalize; (7) ascetic; (8) panders; (9) sublimation; (10) wanton

VI
TRUE OR FALSE?

Are you feeling more and more power and understanding? Try two more exercises to reinforce your learning.

Check your reaction to each statement.

1. Psychoanalysts encourage their patients to *rationalize*.
   True___ False___

2. *Gregarious* people avoid social gatherings.
   True___ False___

3. A haughty person is necessarily *obsequious*.
   True___ False___

4. *Vicarious* experiences are naturally more satisfying than real ones.

    True____ False____

5. Intoxicated people often become *maudlin*.

    True____ False____

6. *Asceticism* is a popular practice among wealthy Americans.

    True____ False____

7. Men of strong ethics and integrity usually *pander* to the desires of others.

    True____ False____

8. *Sublimation* is a self-destructive practice.

    True____ False____

9. During its latter period, Ancient Rome was noted for *wanton* excesses.

    True____ False____

10. One becomes *effete* through self-discipline and careful restraint.

    True____ False____

ANSWERS: All false except 5 and 9.

VII
SAME OR OPPOSITE?

Is each pair of words essentially the same or more nearly opposite in meaning? Check your quick reaction.

1. vicarious—actual

    Same ____ Opposite ____

2. rationalization—justification

    Same ____ Opposite ____

3. gregarious—solitary

    Same ____ Opposite ____

4. obsequious—rude

    Same ____ Opposite ____

5. maudlin—unsentimental
   Same ____ Opposite ____
6. asceticism—luxury
   Same ____ Opposite ____
7. pander—cater
   Same ____ Opposite ____
8. wanton—restrained
   Same ____ Opposite ____
9. effete—vigorous
   Same ____ Opposite ____
10. sublimated—detoured
    Same ____ Opposite ____

ANSWERS: (1) opposite; (2) same; (3) opposite; (4) opposite; (5) opposite; (6) opposite; (7) same; (8) opposite; (9) opposite; (10) same

VIII

Remember this: Once an adult has finished his schooling, he rarely adds more than twenty-five new words to his vocabulary each year thereafter. Already, in one session, you have at least increased your knowledge of these ten words, even though you may have met them before. Therefore, whenever you add ten new words to your vocabulary you have done almost as much as most people do in six months.

Be sure, though, that you *keep* these words. Can you recall all ten of them now without referring to the text? Here they are in random order, with only the initial letters to prod your memory. When you have them all down, check your spelling against the list on page 27 and pronounce them aloud.

1. E _____
2. A _____
3. M _____
4. V _____

5. P_____
6. W_____
7. O_____
8. R_____
9. S_____
10. G_____

X	X	X	X	X	6	7
8	9	10	11	12	13	14
15	16	17	18	19	20	21
22	23	24	25	26	27	28
29	30					

Words About Doctors and Specialists

Of course you know that you have two different kinds of vocabulary, and that one is much larger than the other.

Your *recognition* vocabulary is made up of the words that you can "recognize" and understand when you read them or hear them spoken.

Your *functional* vocabulary includes the words that you recall and use when *you yourself* speak.

Your recognition vocabulary is about three times as large as your functional vocabulary.

If, as an example, you study French and you learn merely to read that language, you will find that you will be unable to speak it because you are practiced only in recognizing the words in print, but not in recalling them when you don't see them.

Or, conversely, if you are taught only to speak French, you will fail when it comes to reading the language because you have not had any practice in understanding or "recognizing" the printed words.

In order to develop both types of vocabulary it is therefore important that you not only *read* the words that are new to you in this book and *write* them down, but that you say them aloud many times, pronouncing them according to the phonetic respelling following each word.

|

In this chapter we discuss the terms for various specialists in the healing professions.

1. The *obstetrician* (ob´-stə-TRISH´-ən) provides care for pregnant women, delivers babies, and gives postnatal attention to mothers. He practices *obstetrics* (ob-STET´-riks). (Almost all *obstetricians* are also *gynecologists*—see word 8, below.)

2. The *pediatrician* (pee´-dee-ə-TRISH´-ən) takes over after the obstetrician. She specializes in the treatment of infants and very young children; she practices *pediatrics* (pee´-dee-AT´-riks).

3. The *podiatrist* (pə-DY´-ə-trist) treats the minor ailments of your feet. He is also called a chiropodist (kə-ROP´-ə-dist). The practice or profession is *podiatry* (pə-DY´-ə-tree) or *chiropody* (kə-ROP´-ə-dee).

4. The *osteopath* (OSS´-tee-ə-path´) works on the theory that diseases arise chiefly from the displacement of bones, with resultant pressure on nerve centers and blood vessels. Hence, her treatment is manipulation of the affected parts. (However, some *osteopaths* also practice general medicine, obstetrics, pediatrics, etc.) She practices *osteopathy* (oss´-tee-OP´-ə-thee).

5. The *ophthalmologist* (off´-thal-MOL´-ə-jist) is a medical doctor and often a trained surgeon who treats the troubles and the diseases of the eyes. He is also called an *oculist* (OK´-yə-list), or, even more popularly, an eye doctor.

6. The *optometrist* (op-TOM´-ə-trist) checks and corrects vision, usually by prescribing and fitting eyeglasses. She practices *optometry* (op-TOM´-ə-tree).

7. The *optician* (op-TISH´-ən) is a technician who grinds lenses to an ophthalmologist's or optometrist's prescription or who makes or sells eyeglasses, binoculars, and other optical instruments.

8. The *gynecologist* (guy´-nə-KOL´-ə-jist; the first syllable may also be pronounced *jine* or *jin*) specializes in the diseases that are peculiar to women. His profession is *gynecology* (guy´-nə-KOL´-ə-jee). (Almost all *gynecologists* also practice *obstetrics,* as noted above.)

9. The *dermatologist* (dur´-mə-TOL´-ə-jist) specializes in diseases of the skin—rash, acne, allergies, lesions, psoriasis, eczema, etc. Her specialty is *dermatology* (dur´-mə-TOL´-ə-jee).

10. The *psychiatrist* (sy-KY´-ə-trist; the first syllable may also be pronounced sə) is a medical specialist in mental ailments, emotional problems, psychoses, neuroses, etc. He practices *psychiatry* (sy-KY´-ə-tree).

11. The *orthodontist* (or´-thə-DON´-tist) specializes in straightening crooked teeth and in correcting bad "bites," or, as they are called in the vocabulary of *orthodontia* (or´-thə-DON´-shə), "malocclusions."

II
WHICH SPECIALIST
WOULD YOU VISIT?

Write the title of the specialist you would suggest for each of the following ailments.

1. You have a painful corn. _____

2. You need eyeglasses. _____

3. Your baby has colic. _____

4. You need a doctor to deliver your baby. _____

5. A friend of yours has had a complete mental collapse. _____

6. A child you know has crooked teeth. _____

7. A woman is suffering from a yeast infection. _____

8. You are troubled with a skin rash. _____

9. You have an eye disease that needs expert attention. _____

10. You have an illness that you believe can be cured by bone manipulation. _____

11. You want new frames for your glasses. _____

ANSWERS: (1) podiatrist *or* chiropodist; (2) optometrist; (3) pediatrician; (4) obstetrician; (5) psychiatrist; (6) orthodontist; (7) gynecologist; (8) dermatologist; (9) ophthalmologist *or* oculist; (10) osteopath; (11) optician

III
TEST YOUR LINGUISTIC INSTINCT

You have studied the titles of eleven specialists and the form that designates the profession or practice of each one. (An *obstetrician* practices *obstetrics,* a *pediatrician* is involved in *pediatrics,* etc.) Can you, now, figure out the *adjective* form of each word that would *describe* the practitioner or his work? For example, the *obstetrician* has *obstetrical* patients.

1. The *pediatrician* has _____ patients.

2. The *podiatrist* has _____ patients.

3. The *osteopath* engages in _____ healing.

4. The *ophthalmologist* does _____ work.

5. The *optometrist* has an _____ practice.

6. The *gynecologist* treats _____ cases.

7. The *dermatologist* treats _____ conditions.

8. The *psychiatrist* handles _____ problems.
9. The *orthodontist* handles _____ problems.
10. The *optician* makes or sells _____ goods.

ANSWERS: (1) pediAT´ric; (2) podiAT´ric; (3) osteoPATH´ic;
(4) ophthalmoLOG´ical; (5) optoMET´ric; (6) gynecoLOG´ical;
(7) dermatoLOG´ical; (8) psychiAT´ric; (9) orthoDON´tic;
(10) OP´tical

IV

IS THERE A DOCTOR IN THE HOUSE?

In a professional building in a large city, you see a number of medical titles on the doors as you go down the halls.

In each case, check the definition or description that fits each title. Before you look at the answers, see if you can name the professions of the two that are left.

Room One: The shingle says "Jane Doe, *Podiatrist*."

a. She treats diseases of the skin.

b. She's the person to see when you have an aching corn.

c. She practices general medicine.

Room Two: The office of Richard Roe, *Psychiatrist*.

a. He treats diseases of the skin.

b. He corrects malocclusions.

c. People who have emotional problems visit him.

Room Three: The office of Sascha Jones, *Ophthalmologist*.

a. She knows all about diseases of the eye and refractive errors, and may resort to surgery, if necessary, to correct eye ailments.

b. She'll check your vision and prescribe glasses if you need them.

c. She'll be happy to sell you any sort of optical instruments—binoculars, telescopes, microscopes.

Room Four: The office of Alex Brown, *Osteopath*.

    a.   Their specialty is the treatment of corns and bunions.

    b.   Holding that diseases arise chiefly from displacement of the bones, with resultant pressure on nerves and blood vessels, they remedy an ailment by manipulation of the affected parts.

    c.   They fill and extract teeth.

Room Five: The name on this door is Stevie Smith, *Obstetrician*.

    a.   She treats diseases and ailments peculiar to old age.

    b.   She specializes in the ills of infancy and childhood.

    c.   She delivers babies.

ANSWERS: (1) b; (a) is a dermatologist, (c) a doctor, physician, or general practitioner; (2) c; (a) is a dermatologist, (b) an orthodontist; (3) a; (b) is an optometrist, (c) an optician; (4) b; (a) is a podiatrist or chiropodist, (c) a dentist; (5) c; (a) is a geriatrician, (b) a pediatrician.

X	X	X	X	X	X	7
8	9	10	11	12	13	14
15	16	17	18	19	20	21
22	23	24	25	26	27	28
29	30					

Verbs Give You Power

Do you remember your old schoolbook definition of a verb? It went something like this: "A verb is that part of speech which asserts, declares, or predicates."

But a dynamic verb is more than this. It is the catalyst of the sentence. It is the word that brings the sentence to life.

Choose your verbs with care.

If you pick a dull verb, your speech will be dull, barely serving its primary purpose of communication, making little impression on the mind of your reader or listener.

A choice of powerful verbs, on the other hand, will make your speech electric, galvanic. Like a powder charge, it can give the impact of bullets to all the other words in your sentence.

A single illustration of this statement will be enough. Which of the two following sentences has the greater force?

1. He is a moral leper; let us keep away from him and
    have nothing to do with him.
2. He is a moral leper; let us *ostracize* him.

The answer is obvious, isn't it? One word has expressed the meaning of ten.

So watch your verbs. They are packed with power.

I

Here are ten dynamic verbs that belong in a rich vocabulary. We are not going to give you their precise definitions. Just read the sentences in which they occur and see if you can guess the meanings of the ones you don't already know. Pronounce them aloud.

What are some of the things people do?

1. They *expiate* (EKS´-pee-ate) their sins, crimes, blunders, or errors.
2. They *importune* (im-pər-TOON´) God for divine favors.
3. They *impute* (im-PYOOT´) unworthy motives to their enemies.
4. They *scintillate* (SIN´-tə-late), the wittier ones, at cocktail parties.
5. They *mulct* (MULKT) the unwary or gullible public.
6. They *ostracize* (OS´-trə-size) members of religious, political, or racial minorities.
7. They *deprecate* (DEP´-rə-kate) the foibles of others.
8. They *procrastinate* (prō-KRAS´-tə-nate) and then vow to be more punctual in the future.
9. They *rusticate* (RUSS´-tə-kate) in the summer time, if finances permit.
10. They *vegetate* (VEJ´-ə-tate) all year, if they are lacking in imagination, initiative, or energy.

II

Referring to Section I, write the proper verb next to its definition. The definitions do not appear in the same order as the sentences above.

1. Live in a passive way _____
2. Deprive of a possession unjustly _____
3. Make amends for _____
4. Beg for ceaselessly; beseech; entreat _____
5. Exclude from public or private favor; ban _____
6. Put off until a future time; delay _____
7. Sparkle with wit or humor _____
8. Spend time in the country _____
9. Ascribe, attribute, or charge an act or thought (to someone), usually in a bad or accusatory sense _____
10. Disapprove of (the actions of someone) _____

ANSWERS: (1) vegetate; (2) mulct; (3) expiate; (4) importune; (5) ostracize; (6) procrastinate; (7) scintillate; (8) rusticate; (9) impute; (10) deprecate

III

Which of the verbs most aptly describes the characteristic action of the following people?

1. He is too indolent to get his work done on time.
   He _____
2. He is accustomed to blaming others.
   He _____
3. He is a sparkling and witty person.
   He _____
4. He is remorseful and wishes to make amends.
   He _____
5. He is a person who is in a rut and leads a monotonous life.
   He _____
6. He is an exclusive individual, avoiding people who are different from himself.
   He _____

7. He cheats others.

He _____

8. He's an insistent beggar.

He _____

9. He looks down on the acts of others.

He _____

10. He is on a vacation in the country.

He _____

ANSWERS: (1) procrastinates; (2) imputes; (3) scintillates; (4) expiates; (5) vegetates; (6) ostracizes; (7) mulcts; (8) importunes; (9) deprecates; (10) rusticates

IV

You will find, below, eleven pairs of sentences. The second sentence of each pair has a blank line that corresponds to an italicized phrase in the first sentence. Write, on this blank line, either another form of, or a noun or adjective derived from, one of the verbs we have studied in this chapter.

1. He has been *spending his time in the country*. He has been _____.

2. Why do you keep *nagging me for favors*? Why are you so _____?

3. He took $1,000,000 from the public *by dishonest methods*. He _____ the public of $1,000,000.

4. *Excluding him from our group* is our most potent weapon against someone who is disloyal. _____ is our most potent weapon against someone who is disloyal.

5. For the past two years, I have been *accomplishing nothing and getting nowhere*. For the past two years, I have been _____.

6. He *showed contempt and disapproval of* the younger generation. He _____ the younger generation.

7. *To make amends for* his sin, he did penance for three days. In _____ of his sin, he did penance for three days.

8. Do they *accuse* me *of committing* these offenses? Have they _____ these offenses to me?

9. I resent your *accusation that* I *committed these offenses.* I resent your _____ of these offenses to me.

10. She is a *sparkling and witty* speaker. She is a _____ speaker.

11. *Putting off till tomorrow* is the thief of time. _____ is the thief of time.

ANSWERS: (1) rusticating; (2) importunate; (3) mulcted; (4) ostracism; (5) vegetating; (6) deprecated; (7) expiation; (8) imputed; (9) imputation; (10) scintillating; (11) procrastination

V

Now for a change of pace, with a few verbal gymnastics for you. Can you think of five verbs ending in *-ate*? They have not appeared in this chapter. The definitions and initial letters are offered to help you.

1. Have control over   D _____
2. Make easier   F _____
3. Follow the example of   E _____
4. Make gestures or motions to convey meanings   G _____
5. Get better   R _____

ANSWERS: (1) dominate (DOM´-ə-nate); (2) facilitate (fə-SIL´-ə-tate); (3) emulate (EM´-yə-late); (4) gesticulate (jess-TIK´-yə-late); (5) recuperate (ree-KOO´-pə-rate)

Now can you think of five verbs ending in *-ize*?

1. Be condescending toward   P _____
2. Make pay a fine or suffer punishment   P _____
3. Make vivid or moving   D _____

4. Make live forever   I _____

5. Appropriate and claim as one's own the literary work of another   P _____

ANSWERS: (1) patronize (PAT´-rə-nize); (2) penalize (PEE´-nə-lize); (3) dramatize (DRAM´-ə-tize); (4) immortalize (i-MORE´-tə-lize); (5) plagiarize (PLAY´-jee-ə-rise)

VI

Can you make the verbs of Section V an active part of your speaking vocabulary? Fill the blanks of the following sentences. Some new form of the verb may be required, such as *dominates, dominating, dominated.*

1. Beethoven's compositions have always _____ the musical scene.

2. Carl Sandburg's biography vividly _____ the life of Lincoln as no other book has ever been able to.

3. I have never seen a sick man _____ so quickly.

4. Your friends think you are conceited because you seem to _____ them.

5. Nature will _____ you for your alcoholic excesses.

6. Let us _____ the habits of successful men.

7. In her confusion, she _____ wildly.

8. He built an insecure and dishonest literary reputation by _____ the classics.

9. Let me pack for you; that will _____ your departure.

10. The "Elegy in a Country Churchyard" did much to _____ the poet Thomas Gray.

ANSWERS: (1) dominated; (2) dramatizes; (3) recuperate; (4) patronize; (5) penalize; (6) emulate; (7) gesticulated; (8) plagiarizing; (9) facilitate; (10) immortalize

VII

Twenty dynamic verbs, excellent additions to a powerful vocabulary, have been discussed in this chapter. How many of them can you call to mind? Let us put your learning and retention to a test.

In order to prompt your memory, the initial letters are given. Recall and write down as many as you can before referring to the preceding pages to check yourself. A score of twelve out of twenty is fair, fifteen good, eighteen or nineteen excellent, all twenty superb.

1. E _____
2. I _____
3. I _____
4. S _____
5. M _____
6. O _____
7. D _____
8. P _____
9. R _____
10. V _____
11. D _____
12. F _____
13. E _____
14. G _____
15. R _____
16. P _____
17. P _____
18. D _____
19. I _____
20. P _____

For the next few days keep your eyes and ears alert for verbs. Note them as you read, or as people speak to you. See whether they are effective and do their work. Billboards, posters, and other advertisements will be particularly helpful, for advertising space costs money and the publicity people have to pick their verbs with care. As you read your newspaper, watch for examples of well-chosen, dynamic verbs.

Take care of your verbs. They will add power, color, and punch to your speech and writing.

X	X	X	X	X	X	X
8	9	10	11	12	13	14
15	16	17	18	19	20	21
22	23	24	25	26	27	28
29	30					

Words About Theories

The mentally alert person is not content to live merely from day to day, completely circumscribed by such things as food, money, clothing, and entertainment. Occasionally they are tempted to speculate on *why* they are living and what the controlling forces of their life are. This chapter deals with a few of the terms that are applied to these motivating forces by different people who have varying points of view.

1. Is there a God? Nothing so closely approaches the outer limits of abstraction as theorizing about a supernatural and supreme being. Many of us worship, most of us at least accept, some form of deity. Do you belong to the minority who insist, often belligerently, that man makes God in his own image, that God is a figment of the imagination and hence completely, irrevocably nonexistent? Then you are an *atheist* (AY´-thee-ist; *th* as in *think*) and your philosophy is called *atheism* (AY´-thee-iz-əm). The word is from the Greek *a*, "without," and *theos*, "god."

2. To many other thinkers it seems more reasonable to say that the existence or nonexistence of a supreme being is one mystery the human mind will never fathom. How did the world come into being? How did

life begin? Is there a father who looks after his children, or are we the products of purposeless chance? Do you answer these questions by saying that no one knows and no one can ever hope to know? Then you are an *agnostic* (ag-NOSS´-tik), and your doctrine is called *agnosticism* (ag-NOSS´-tə-siz-əm). This word, too, is from the Greek, derived from *agnostos,* "not knowing."

3. Why did that young child dart across the roadway just as a huge truck rounded the bend? How do you explain the needless snuffing out of an innocent life? Is it due to blind chance? To cause and effect? Why should some great benefactor of humanity be cut off in his prime? Are such events controlled by accident? Or are they determined by fate? (*Fate,* incidentally, is derived from the Latin *fatus,* "spoken" or "predicted.")

If you believe that everything that happens is predetermined, foreordained, written down, as it were, on the far-off pages of some mighty volume, you are a *fatalist* (FAY´-tə-list) and your theory is called *fatalism* (FAY´-tə-liz-əm).

4. In this world of ours you will find some people who think only of themselves and of their own selfish advantage, and who actually maintain that all virtue consists in the pursuit of self-interest. Completely indifferent to the needs, feelings, or wishes of others, they base their actions on personal gain and direct benefit. They believe in, and are motivated by, *egoism* (EE´-gō-iz-əm); a member of such a cult is an *egoist* (EE´-gō-ist). (These words, characteristically, derive from the Latin *ego,* "I.")

5. If your characteristics are opposite to those of an egoist, if you have an unselfish regard for, and devotion to, the interests and needs of others, then you are an *altruist* (AL´-trōō-ist) and you practice *altruism* (AL´trōō-iz-əm). The relationship of this word to the Latin *alter,* "other," is clear.

6. Can you rise above petty considerations of pleasure and pain, joy and grief? Can you meet adversity with indifference and submit to the

arrows and slings of misfortune with a dignified resignation? Can you give up envy, greed, jealousy, hatred, and other human passions? Can you suffer mental and physical pain without complaint? If you can honestly say "yes" to these questions, and if you sincerely believe that such self-control makes for a better way of life, then you are a *stoic* (STŌ´ik), a practitioner of *stoicism* (STŌ´-ə-siz-əm). The founder of *stoicism* was the Greek philosopher Zeno, who lived about three hundred years before Christ. *Stoic* is from the Greek *stoikos,* which, in turn, is from *stoa,* "porch." Zeno taught in the Stoa Poikile, or "Painted Porch," in Athens.

7. Are you apt to say: "No other nation can hold a candle to my country. We are the supermen, the chosen people. Every other race is inferior to mine and they are all destined to be our slaves when the day comes"? This is not patriotism. Or, rather, it is patriotism carried to an illogical and ludicrous extreme. If you happen to talk this way, you are a *chauvinist* (SHŌ´-və-nist); you are addicted to *chauvinism* (SHŌ´-və-niz-əm). These terms come from the name of a real man, Nicolas Chauvin of Rochefort, who was so demonstrative in his devotion to Napoleon and to the imperial cause that he was ridiculed on the French stage at the time.

8. Are you a braggart about your country's power? Do you always want your nation to use force? Do you want to call out the Army, Navy, and Air Force on the slightest provocation, and send our soldiers and sailors around the world to show those "damn foreigners" who's the boss? "Do the other nations want war?" you ask. "We'll give it to them. And if they don't want it, we'll give it to them anyway." If this is a description of your philosophy, you are a *jingoist* (JING´-gō-ist), and your heart beats in tune with the martial music of *jingoism* (JING´-gō-iz-əm). (The "Jingoes" were originally a section of the Conservative party in England in 1877 who were eager to have their nation support the Turks in the Russo-Turkish war.)

9. Is it best that our government follow the political faith, methods, and tenets of our fathers and grandfathers, or shall we move rapidly ahead,

change constantly, explore and experiment? Those who believe in *liberalism* follow the latter philosophy. They owe allegiance to no party, are independent in thought and action, and are always anathema to those who wish the government to pursue the well-trodden paths. *Liberals* prefer a changing, dynamic, experimenting government. They vote for progress, sometimes in the sense that anything new and different and previously untried is progressive. The Romans gave us the word *liber,* "free."

10. The *conservative,* on the other hand, is opposed to change. He believes that what is, is best. He prefers that his government follow familiar, tried, tested, and safe policies. "We're content with what we have," he says. "Why take the risk of sailing into uncharted waters?" The word derives from Latin *conservare,* "to preserve." (An extreme *liberal* is a *radical*; an extreme *conservative* is a *reactionary.*)

11. What type of life is best? To one group of thinkers, such a question has a simple answer. That life is the most successful, says the *epicurean* (ep´-ə-kyŏŏ-REE´-ən), which brings to each person the maximum of pleasure and the minimum of pain. The doctrine of *epicureanism* (ep´-ə-kyŏŏ-REE´-ə-niz-əm) teaches that pleasure is the chief good. (*Epicurean* should not be confused with *epicure,* one who enjoys the delights of the table and who is expert and fastidious in his choice of food.)

Ready for a check on your learning and retention?

I

What philosophy is expressed by each of the statements below?

1. "I'm interested in the welfare of the other fellow, not in my own."   A _____

2. "Let the other fellow take care of himself. My interests come first, last, and always."   E _____

3. "Mine is the superior race. Have we not the monopoly on beauty, strength, brains, creativeness, honesty, virtue, and bravery?"   C _____

4. "Let's not stand still in politics. Progress, change, experimentation—that's what we need!"   L _____

5. "Happiness, pleasure, fun, revelry: these are the most important things in life."   E _____

6. "There's a God? Don't be silly. Only stupid people believe in God."   A _____

7. "Maybe there is a God. Maybe there isn't. I don't know, and I don't believe anybody else does or ever will."
   A _____

8. "The wise and brave man is indifferent to both pain and pleasure."   S _____

9. "We'll build up our nuclear power, our troops, and our navy; we'll arm to the hilt. Then we'll dare any nation in the world to knock the chip off our shoulder!"
   J _____

10. "You can't change the future. It's all planned and written down."   F _____

11. "Let's keep things just as they are. We're getting along all right, so why fool around with any dangerous half-baked, new-fangled theories?"   C _____

ANSWERS: (1) altruist; (2) egoist; (3) chauvinist; (4) liberal; (5) epicurean; (6) atheist; (7) agnostic; (8) stoic; (9) jingoist; (10) fatalist; (11) conservative

II

Adjective forms of these nouns are as follows:

NOUN	ADJECTIVE
altruism	altruistic
atheism	atheistic
agnosticism	agnostic
fatalism	fatalistic
egoism	egoistic

stoicism	stoical
chauvinism	chauvinistic
jingoism	jingoistic
liberalism	liberal
conservatism	conservative
epicureanism	epicurean

Can you fit the correct adjective in each of the following phrases or sentences?

1. The _____ attitude of the ungodly.
2. The _____ doubts of the skeptical.
3. Age tends to bring a _____ tinge to one's politics.
4. Politically, youth is inclined to be _____.
5. The _____ belief of the Mandate of Heaven in China.
6. The narrow, _____ desires of the conceited.
7. The _____ resignation of those who have suffered much.
8. The _____ blatancy of professional "flag-wavers."
9. The _____ desires of the self-indulgent.
10. Threats, "saber-rattling," and a call-up of the reserves have often been the _____ means by which strong nations have imposed their will on their weaker neighbors.
11. The _____ attitudes of most parents to their children.

ANSWERS: (1) atheistic; (2) agnostic; (3) conservative; (4) liberal; (5) fatalistic; (6) egoistic; (7) stoical; (8) chauvinistic; (9) epicurean; (10) jingoistic; (11) altruistic

III

Finally, to make these words an integral part of your thinking and speaking vocabulary, try this exercise. Can you react immediately to each statement as either essentially *true* or generally *false*? Read each statement quickly, once only, then check at once the answer you trust.

1. The *altruist* hates people.
   True____ False____

2. An *atheist* is a steady churchgoer.
   True____ False____

3. The *agnostic* is deeply religious.
   True____ False____

4. A *fatalist* never takes chances.
   True____ False____

5. An *egoist* wants to help his peer.
   True____ False____

6. The *stoic* becomes hysterical under the stress of tragedy or disaster.
   True____ False____

7. *Chauvinists* often switch their allegiance to other nations.
   True____ False____

8. A *jingoist* is interested in peace at any cost.
   True____ False____

9. A political *liberal* shies away from innovation.
   True____ False____

10. A political *conservative* believes in greatly enhanced Federal power.
    True____ False____

11. An *epicurean* pursues a life of austerity and self-denial.
    True____ False____

ANSWERS: All statements, of course, are outrageously false.

✗	✗	✗	✗	✗	✗	✗
✗	9	10	11	12	13	14
15	16	17	18	19	20	21
22	23	24	25	26	27	28
29	30					

Quick Vocabulary Builder

English is a reservoir of the classical languages. It has taken over to itself and has absorbed for its own use more than 25 percent of the Greek language and more than 50 percent of the Latin language. It is obvious, then, that a knowledge of Greek and Latin roots is invaluable in any program of vocabulary building.

In the exercises ahead we will take English words apart and will show how you can easily identify and understand scores of words that you may never have seen before.

I

1. *Monogamy* (mə-NOG´-ə-mee). A one-to-one system of marriage; a man or woman has only one current spouse at any time. From Greek *monos*, "one," *gamos*, "marriage."

2. *Bigamy* (BIG´-ə-mee). Involvement by one person in two or more concurrent marriages. From Latin *bis*, "twice" or "two," plus *gamos*.

3. *Polygamy* (pə-LIG´-ə-mee). A custom, once prevalent among the

Mormons in Utah and encountered today in some parts of Asia, Africa, the Near East, etc., in which a man has more than one wife. The first part of the word is from Greek *polys,* "many."

4. *Misogamy* (mə-SOG´-ə-mee). Hatred of marriage. From Greek *misein,* "to hate," plus *gamos.*

II

Notice how the Greek and Latin roots discussed in the previous section lead to four new words.

1. *Monotheism* (MON´-ə-thee-iz´-əm). The belief in a single, supreme deity. Greek *monos,* "one," combined with *theos,* "god."

2. *Bicuspid* (by-KUS´-pid). A tooth with two prongs. Latin *bis,* "twice" or "two," and *cuspis,* "point."

3. *Polyglot* (POL´-ee-glot´). *Glotta* is Greek for "tongue"; the *polyglot* is one who speaks many tongues or languages.

4. *Misanthropy* (mə-SAN´-thrə-pee). *Anthropos* is Greek for "man." We have, then, the hatred of man or of mankind. A *misanthrope* (MISS´-ən-thrope), therefore, is anyone who has a morbid aversion to, or distrust of, his peers.

III

Let us take a quick review of the roots we've discovered so far. Can you remember the meaning of each word using these roots?

1. *Monos* (Greek), "one," as in *monogamy* and *monotheism*
2. *Gamos* (Greek), "marriage," as in *monogamy, bigamy, misogamy,* and *polygamy*
3. *Bis* (Latin), "twice" or "two," as in *bigamy* and *bicuspid*
4. *Polys* (Greek), "many," as in *polygamy* and *polyglot*
5. *Misein* (Greek), "to hate," as in *misogamy* and *misanthropy*
6. *Theos* (Greek), "god," as in *monotheism, bitheism,* and *polytheism*
7. *Cuspis* (Latin), "point," as in *bicuspid*

8. *Glotta* (Greek), "tongue," as in *polyglot*

9. *Anthropos* (Greek), "man," as in *misanthropy*

IV

Now on to further explorations into roots:

1. *Theology* (thee-OL´-ə-jee). The study of God and religion. To *theos* we add the Greek root *logos*, "knowledge," "study," or "word."

2. *Philanthropy* (fə-LAN´-thrə-pee). Love of mankind. The root *anthropos* is combined with the Greek *philein*, "to love." A *philanthropist* (fə-LAN´-thrə-pist), then, who gives money to the poor, is literally a "lover of his peers."

3. *Anthropology* (an´-thrō-POL´-ə-jee). Study of man, i.e., science of human development and history—a combination of *anthropos* and *logos*.

4. *Philology* (fe-LOL´-ə-jee). Study of language, i.e., science of linguistics—literally, a love of words, from *philein* combined with *logos*.

V

Ready for a test of your knowledge of Greek and Latin roots? Write the meaning of each root in the appropriate blank below, then give one example of an English word based on this root.

ROOT	MEANING	EXAMPLE
1. *bis*	_____	_____
2. *theos*	_____	_____
3. *philein*	_____	_____
4. *misein*	_____	_____
5. *gamos*	_____	_____
6. *glotta*	_____	_____
7. *monos*	_____	_____
8. *cuspis*	_____	_____
9. *polys*	_____	_____

10. *anthropos* _____ _____

11. *logos* _____ _____

ANSWERS: (1) twice, two; (2) god; (3) love; (4) hate; (5) marriage;
(6) tongue; (7) one; (8) point; (9) many; (10) man, mankind;
(11) study, knowledge, word

To check your examples, refer to previous pages.

VI

Can you qualify as a word detective? Keep in mind the eleven roots we
have discussed and try to arrive at the meanings of the italicized words.
Guess intelligently, referring to previous explanations as often as you
wish to. Write your meaning in the blank line following each sentence.

1. Some scholars wear a *monocle* (MON´-ə-kəl).

_____

2. He delivered an interesting *monologue* (MON´-ə-log´).

_____

3. He has a *monopoly* of the coffee market (mə-NOP´-ə-lee).

_____

4. He lives in a *monastery* (MON´-ə-stair´-ee).

_____

5. He is riding a *bicycle* (BY´-sə-kol).

_____

6. Man is a *biped* (BY´-ped).

_____

7. France and England made a *bilateral* (by-LAT´-ə-rəl)
   agreement.

_____

8. A rectangle is a *polygon* (POL´-ee-gon´).

_____

9. A *misogynist* (mə-SAHJ´-ə-nist) shuns the company
   of women.

_____

10. Romans practiced *polytheism* (POL´-ee-thee-iz´-əm).

11. This tooth is a *tricuspid* (try-KUS´-pid).

12. The president's wonderful stamp collection is the envy of *philatelists* (fə-LAT´-ə-lists).

13. The *anthropoid* (AN´-thrə-poid´) apes are similar in appearance to humans.

14. *Biology* (by-OL´-ə-jee) is a fascinating science.

15. England is a *monarchy* (MON´-ər-kee).

ANSWERS: (1) lens for *one* eye; (2) speech by *one* person; (3) control by *one* person (of the market); (4) place where people live *alone*; (5) vehicle of *two* wheels; (6) creature with *two* feet; (7) *two*-sided; (8) *many*-sided figure; (9) *hater* of women; (10) belief in *many* gods; (11) tooth with three *points*; (12) *lovers*, hence collectors, of stamps; (13) *manlike*; (14) *study* of life; (15) country where *one* person rules

VII

Consider, perhaps with amazement, how many new words you have learned in a very short time by tracing them back to their Latin or Greek derivations. Pronounce each aloud as you come to it, and review briefly its meaning as reflected by the root structure.

1. *gamos*, marriage
    monogamy (mə-NOG´-ə-mee)
    bigamy (BIG´-ə-mee)
    polygamy (pə-LIG´-ə-mee)
    misogamy (mə-SOG´-ə-mee)

2. *monos,* one
   monotheism (MON´-ə-thee-iz´-əm)
   monogamy (mə-NOG´-ə-mee)
   monocle (MON´-ə-kəl)
   monologue (MON´-ə-log´)
   monopoly (mə-NOP´-ə-lee)
   monastery (MON´-ə-stair´-ee)
   monarchy (MON´-ər-kee)

3. *bis,* twice, two
   bicuspid (by-KUS´-pid)
   bicycle (BY´-sə-kol)
   biped (BY´-ped)
   bilateral (by-LAT´-ə-rəl)
   bigamous (BIG´-ə-məs)

4. *polys,* many
   polygamy (pə-LIG´-ə-mee)
   polyglot (POL´-ee-glot´)
   polygon (POL´-ee-gon´)
   polytheism (POL´-ee-thee-iz´-əm)

5. *misein,* to hate
   misogamy (mə-SOG´-ə-mee)
   misogynist (mə-SAHJ´-ə-nist)
   misanthropy (mə-SAN´-thrə-pee)

6. *theos,* god
   theology (thee-OL´-ə-jee)
   monotheist (MON´-ə-thee-ist)

7. *logos,* word, study, knowledge
   biology (by-OL´-ə-jee)
   theology (thee-OL´-ə-jee)
   philology (fə-LOL´-ə-jee)
   anthropology (an´-thrō-POL´-ə-jee)

8. *philein,* to love
   philologist (fə-LOL´-ə-jist)
   philatelist (fə-LAT´-ə-list)
   philanthropy (fə-LAN´-thrə-pee)

9. *anthropos,* man, mankind
   anthropoid (AN´-thrə-poid)
   anthropologist (an-thrə-POL´-ə-jist)
   philanthropist (fə-LAN´-thrə-pist)
   misanthrope (MISS´-ən-thrope)
   misanthropist (mis-AN´-thrə-pist)

10. *cuspis,* point
    bicuspid (by-KUS´-pid)
    tricuspid (try-KUS´-pid)

11. *glotta,* tongue
    polyglot (POL´-ee-glot´)

VIII

Final review time! If you feel a happy and secure control of the material of this chapter, try this simple test, in which you have to fill in one or more blanks in each sentence. Can you make a perfect score without referring to previous information?

1. One who practices *monogamy* has only one _____.
2. A *misogamist* _____ marriage.
3. *Theology* is the study of _____ or _____.
4. *Biology* is the _____ of life.
5. A *philatelist* collects _____.
6. A *misanthropist* _____ mankind.
7. *Anthropology* is the science of _____ development.
8. A *bicuspid* has _____ points.
9. A *tricuspid* has _____ points.

10. *Anthropoid* means "similar to, or in the form of, a
    _____."

11. A *polyglot* speaks _____ languages.

12. A *polygon* has _____ sides.

13. Under *polygamy,* a man may have _____ wives.

14. In America, a *bigamous* marriage is _____.

15. In a *monotheistic* religion, there is only one _____.

16. A *biped* has two _____.

17. A two-wheeled vehicle is a _____.

18. An agreement endorsed by two sides is called _____.

19. A lens for only one eye is called a _____.

20. A speech by one person is a _____.

21. Control of the market by one person or group is a

    _____.

22. A place where men live in seclusion is a _____.

23. A nation which has one, usually hereditary, ruler is a

    _____.

24. Belief in many gods is called _____.

25. A *misogynist* hates _____.

ANSWERS: (1) spouse, wife, husband; (2) hates; (3) God, religion;
(4) study, science; (5) stamps; (6) hates; (7) human, man's, mankind's;
(8) two; (9) three; (10) human, human being, man, person, etc.;
(11) many; (12) many; (13) many; (14) illegal, unlawful, etc.;
(15) God; (16) legs, feet; (17) bicycle; (18) bilateral; (19) monocle;
(20) monologue; (21) monopoly; (22) monastery; (23) monarchy;
(24) polytheism; (25) women, females, etc.

✗	✗	✗	✗	✗	✗	✗
✗	✗	10	11	12	13	14
15	16	17	18	19	20	21
22	23	24	25	26	27	28
29	30					

A Quick Test of Your Progress to Date

You are of course aware that you will never add very rapidly to your vocabulary by merely being *exposed* to words, or by reading, or by talking. *You must have a plan.*

Here is one way to get ahead with words in everyday life. It's the simplest thing in the world.

Buy a small pocket notebook. When you read a newspaper, a magazine, or a book, or listen to TV or the radio, and come upon a strange word, enter it in your notebook. Then look it up in the dictionary. If you find that it's some abstruse or highly technical term, such as, say, *syzygy*, "an immovable union between two brachials of a crinoid," just pass it by. You won't be using it unless you are studying to be a professor of biology. But if it sounds like a word that will be helpful to you, take possession of it, make it your own personal property. Say it aloud many times. Study its definition, note its derivation. Be sure, also, to copy from the dictionary the sample sentence in which it is used, if such is given. Then write your own sentence along the lines of the example in the dictionary.

All this will take only a few minutes or so, but it is necessary to make the practice a daily habit. Then the list in your notebook will grow and grow, as will your command of English.

We want, at this point, to help you gain complete possession of any of the words in the first eight chapters that may have once been unfamiliar to you.

In this review, you have, as usual, the responsibility of grading yourself. After you have compared your answers with those given at the end of the chapter, we will give you an interpretation of your score and you can then see what progress you have made.

I

1. The study of the origins of words or of word histories is called
   (a) philology; (b) verbology; (c) etymology
2. The "taxicabs" in Ancient Rome gave rise to our word
   (a) calculate; (b) supercilious; (c) captain
3. The Greek syllable *graph* means
   (a) seeing; (b) writing; (c) speaking
4. The word *run* has approximately _____ different dictionary meanings.
   (a) 3; (b) 20; (c) 90
5. Some words require emotional maturity to be understood.
   (a) True? *or* (b) False?

II

Each phrase in column B defines a word in column A. Match the two columns.

A	B
1. *vicarious*	a. appeal to the baser emotions
2. *rationalize*	b. tearfully sentimental
3. *gregarious*	c. company-loving

4. *obsequious*   d. second-hand or substitutional in experience

5. *maudlin*   e. fawning and servile

6. *ascetic*   f. justify, usually unconsciously (an unworthy act)

7. *pander*   g. severely self-denying

8. *sublimate*   h. refine; turn into higher or socially acceptable channels

9. *wanton*   i. worn out; sterile; exhausted from rich or overindulgent living

10. *effete*   j. unrestrained

III

Check the correct forms:

1. The *obstetrician:*
   (a) delivers babies; (b) treats babies; (c) treats women's diseases

2. The *osteopath:*
   (a) straightens teeth; (b) specializes in skin diseases;
   (c) treats diseases by manipulating the bones

3. The *optometrist:*
   (a) sells lenses; (b) measures your eyes for glasses;
   (c) operates on your eyes

4. The *podiatrist:*
   (a) treats foot ailments; (b) treats mental ailments;
   (c) treats nerve ailments

5. The *psychiatrist* is interested in:
   (a) your stomach; (b) your mind; (c) your eyes

IV

Write the required verb:

1. To stagnate   V_____
2. To postpone   P_____

3. To cheat; to deprive fraudulently   M _____
4. To exclude; to ban   O _____
5. To atone for   E _____
6. To entreat   I _____
7. To sparkle   S _____
8. To disapprove of   D _____
9. To spend time in the country   R _____
10. To charge (someone with)   I _____

V

Fill in each blank space with the type of person who would be most apt to make such a statement.

1. "I have good taste in foods and wines."   E _____
2. "Government should experiment."   L _____
3. "Government must not experiment."   C _____
4. "If they don't want war, give it to them anyway."   J _____
5. "My country is the only one worth anything."   CH _____
6. "Pain will never make me wince."   S _____
7. "The other fellow comes first."   A _____
8. "I come first above all."   E _____
9. "There is no God."   A _____
10. "I don't know whether or not there is a God."   A _____
11. "Everything will happen as it will, no matter what we do."   F _____

VI

Give the meaning of each of the following Greek or Latin roots:

1. *logos*   _____
2. *theos*   _____
3. *bis*   _____
4. *philein*   _____
5. *misein*   _____

6. *monos* _____
7. *anthropos* _____
8. *polys* _____
9. *gamos* _____
10. *cuspis* _____
11. *glotta* _____

ANSWERS:

I: (1) c; (2) a; (3) b; (4) c; (5) a
Scoring: Two points each

Your Score: _____

II: (1) d; (2) f; (3) c; (4) e; (5) b; (6) g; (7) a; (8) h; (9) j; (10) i
Scoring: Two points each

Your Score: _____

III: (1) a; (2) c; (3) b; (4) a; (5) b
Scoring: Two points each

Your Score: _____

IV: (1) vegetate; (2) procrastinate; (3) mulct; (4) ostracize; (5) expiate;
(6) importune; (7) scintillate; (8) deprecate; (9) rusticate; (10) impute
Scoring: Two points each

Your Score: _____

V: (1) epicure; (2) liberal; (3) conservative; (4) jingoist; (5) chauvinist;
(6) stoic; (7) altruist; (8) egoist; (9) atheist; (10) agnostic; (11) fatalist
Scoring: Two points each

Your Score: _____

VI: (1) word, knowledge, study; (2) god; (3) twice, two; (4) love;
(5) hate; (6) one; (7) man, mankind; (8) many; (9) marriage; (10) point;
(11) tongue
Scoring: Two points each

Your Score: _____

Maximum Score: 104

Your Total Score: _____

WHAT YOUR SCORE MEANS

58   or under suggests the possibility that you may not be
            thorough enough as you go along. Work harder; review
            more frequently! Try to improve your score on the next
            general test of your progress.

60–70   is an average and acceptable score. Can you do still better
            next time?

72–86   shows better-than-average learning. Continue building
            your word power and no doors will ever be closed to you.
            Can you, nevertheless, improve your score next time?

88–104   indicates remarkable progress. Your interest and self-
            motivation are high, and your rewards from this work
            will therefore be great.

X	X	X	X	X	X	X
X	X	X	11	12	13	14
15	16	17	18	19	20	21
22	23	24	25	26	27	28
29	30					

Words About Your Peers

We have now a wide and most important group of words to consider. These are the words that describe and catalog a few of the various groups of people and that identify some of their activities. And here is a helpful game that you might like to try. Just jot down on the margins of these pages, opposite each of the twenty-five words that follow, the name of a friend of yours or a well-known actor or public character who, you believe, would best personify the particular word under discussion. Dramatizing the word in this fashion will help fix its meaning in your mind.

You will meet some familiar words in this list, words that we have introduced in previous chapters. But repetition is a part of learning, and very often, when a word appears a second time, it will be presented in another form and with a considerably enriched meaning.

Let us look over a few of the words that characterize the varied types of personalities who inhabit our interesting world.

I

1. The *coquette* (kō-KET´). This girl promises much, flirts egregiously, and delivers very little.
2. The *Circe* (SUR´-see). Her greatest pleasure comes from luring men to their destruction.
3. The *amazon* (AM´-ə-zon´). She's a strong, athletic, headstrong kind of person.
4. The *virago* (və-RAY´-gō). She is the loudmouthed, turbulent, battle-axe type; a vicious nag and scold.
5. The *adonis* (ə-DON´-əs). He's the handsome, Greek-god type who makes the hearts of young girls flutter.

II

1. The *judas* (JOO´-dəs). Don't trust him. He's the traitor who will sell out his best friend for money.
2. The *futilitarian* (fyoo-til´-ə-TAIR´-ee-ən). The pessimist and cynic who sees no particular point to anything in life.
3. The *vulgarian* (vul-GAIR´-ee-ən). He has vulgar tastes and manners.
4. The *pedant* (PED´-ənt). His greatest delight is making an unnecessary show of his learning, especially by correcting petty errors. He attaches exaggerated importance to minute and minor details of scholarship.
5. The *egoist* (EE´-gō-ist.) His credo is selfishness. His interests come first, and no one else matters.
6. The *ascetic* (a-SET´-ik). He lives a severely temperate life and avoids human pleasures and vices.
7. The *esthete* (ESS´-theet). He is a person of fine taste and artistic flair. Hence, he is most responsive to, and delighted with, whatever is beautiful.

III

1. The *demagogue* (DEM´-ə-gog´). By appealing to the prejudices and hatreds of the population, he foments social discontent in order to further his own political ambitions.
2. The *martinet* (mar´-tə-NET´). He's fanatic in his insistence on blind discipline from his subordinates, and a tiresome stickler for form and etiquette.
3. The *sycophant* (SIK´-ə-fənt). By insincere flattery and pretended servility, he hopes to make rich or influential people think of him kindly, especially when they have some crumbs to throw.

IV

1. The *atheist* (AY´-thee-ist). He's sure God is nonexistent.
2. The *agnostic* (ag-NOSS´-tik). He maintains that the human mind is incapable of penetrating the mystery of divine existence. Perhaps there is a God, perhaps not. No man knows.

V

1. The *tyro* (TY´-rō). He's a beginner in some profession, occupation, or art.
2. The *virtuoso* (vur´-choō-Ō´-sō). He is the antithesis of the tyro, having reached the greatest heights of skill and competence in music, painting, or any one of the fine arts.
3. The *philologist* (fə-LOL´-ə-jist). He's a scholar of language and speech.
4. The *clairvoyant* (klair-VOY´-ənt). He claims the ability

to see things not visible to those with normal sight. Hence, he often makes prophecies about the future.

VI

1. The *philatelist* (fə-LAT´-ə-list). He's the stamp collector.
2. The *numismatist* (nŏŏ-MIZ´-mə-tist). He's the coin collector.

VII

1. The *gourmet* (gŏŏr-MAY´). He is knowledgeable and fastidious about eating and drinking, devoting himself to excellent food, special wines, exotic seasonings, etc.
2. The *connoisseur* (kon´-ə-SUR´). He is a critical judge of excellence in the arts, food, drink, etc.

VIII
TEST YOUR LEARNING

Can you fill the blank line with the word that fits each description?

1. He does not believe in God.   A _____
2. He is a skillful practitioner of some art.   V _____
3. He collects rare coins.   N _____
4. He has an unusual appreciation of beauty.   E _____
5. He is ostentatious about his learning.   P _____
6. He will betray a friend.   J _____
7. She is a flirt.   C _____
8. She is a destructive siren.   C _____
9. He is an offensive stickler for discipline.   M _____
10. He lives only for himself.   E _____
11. He lives a simple and austere existence.   A _____
12. He bootlicks the rich and powerful.   S _____
13. He is a false leader of the common people.   D _____

14. He's not sure whether or not God exists.   A _____
15. He claims that life is completely futile.   F _____
16. She's big and muscular.   A _____
17. She has a sharp tongue and a vicious temper.   V _____
18. He has good taste in food.   G _____
19. He's extremely handsome.   A _____
20. He's coarse and uncouth.   V _____
21. He's a beginner in his profession.   T _____
22. He's a student of words.   PH _____
23. He says he can see things that you can't.   C _____
24. He's an authoritative judge and critic in some fine art or other area of excellence.   C _____
25. He collects stamps.   PH _____

ANSWERS: (1) atheist; (2) virtuoso; (3) numismatist; (4) esthete; (5) pedant; (6) judas; (7) coquette; (8) Circe; (9) martinet; (10) egoist; (11) ascetic; (12) sycophant; (13) demagogue; (14) agnostic; (15) futilitarian; (16) amazon; (17) virago; (18) gourmet; (19) adonis; (20) vulgarian; (21) tyro; (22) philologist; (23) clairvoyant; (24) connoisseur; (25) philatelist

IX
REINFORCE YOUR KNOWLEDGE

Ready for another try at the same words? Check the one adjective out of three offered that most nearly fits each noun.

1. *coquette*   sincere, flirtatious, talkative
2. *Circe*   untrustworthy, unapproachable, nagging
3. *amazon*   feminine, alluring, big
4. *virago*   fierce, docile, feminine
5. *adonis*   feminine, good-looking, wasteful
6. *judas*   untrustworthy, unapproachable, unassuming
7. *futilitarian*   optimistic, pessimistic, indifferent

8. *vulgarian* courteous, crude, clever

9. *pedant* corrective, sentimental, soft-hearted

10. *egoist* ambitious, boring, self-centered

11. *ascetic* puny, puerile, puritanical

12. *esthete* talkative, tasteful, triumphant

13. *demagogue* traitorous, troublemaking, temperate

14. *martinet* reckless, easygoing, demanding

15. *sycophant* sincere, hypocritical, handsome

16. *atheist* irreligious, youthful, flattering

17. *agnostic* god-fearing, skeptical, ambitious

18. *tyro* expert, uncouth, unskillful

19. *virtuoso* skilled, indifferent, alluring

20. *philologist* selfish, ill-mannered, scholarly

21. *clairvoyant* prophetic, protesting, fearful

22. *philatelist* stamp-involved, coin-involved, book-involved

23. *numismatist* stamp-involved, coin-involved, book-involved

24. *gourmet* fastidious, vulgar, piggish

25. *connoisseur* discriminating, ignorant, ambitious

ANSWERS: (1) flirtatious; (2) untrustworthy; (3) big; (4) fierce; (5) good-looking; (6) untrustworthy; (7) pessimistic; (8) crude; (9) corrective; (10) self-centered; (11) puritanical; (12) tasteful; (13) troublemaking; (14) demanding; (15) hypocritical; (16) irreligious; (17) skeptical; (18) unskillful; (19) skilled; (20) scholarly; (21) prophetic; (22) stamp-involved; (23) coin-involved; (24) fastidious; (25) discriminating

X
FURTHER REINFORCEMENT

Every time you test your learning and correct your errors or misconceptions you nail down a little more securely your familiarity with these colorful words. In this final test, therefore, you should be so nearly expert that you can make a perfect, or nearly perfect, score. Can you meet the challenge?

Choose the letter of the area from Column II that each person in Column I is involved in. We have added an extra word in Column II to make it more difficult.

I	II
1. *coquette*	a. strength
2. *Circe*	b. uselessness
3. *amazon*	c. obedience
4. *virago*	d. austere existence
5. *adonis*	e. preciseness
6. *judas*	f. skepticism
7. *futilitarian*	g. gaining experience
8. *vulgarian*	h. all beauty
9. *pedant*	i. stamps
10. *egoist*	j. language
11. *ascetic*	k. destruction of males
12. *esthete*	l. insincere flattery
13. *demagogue*	m. political power
14. *martinet*	n. marriage
15. *sycophant*	o. flirting
16. *atheist*	p. coarseness
17. *agnostic*	q. top performance
18. *tyro*	r. self-interest
19. *virtuoso*	s. extrasensory perception
20. *philologist*	t. food
21. *clairvoyant*	u. betrayal
22. *philatelist*	v. high quality
23. *numismatist*	w. male beauty
24. *gourmet*	x. coins
25. *connoisseur*	y. godlessness
	z. nagging

ANSWERS: (1) o; (2) k; (3) a; (4) z; (5) w; (6) u; (7) b; (8) p; (9) e; (10) r; (11) d; (12) h; (13) m; (14) c; (15) l; (16) y; (17) f; (18) g; (19) q; (20) j; (21) s; (22) i; (23) x; (24) t; (25) v

We have discussed with you, and thoroughly tested you on, twenty-five intensely human words about human characteristics, professions, avocations, philosophies, and attitudes. These words are dynamic, meaningful, warm to the touch, pulsating with life. They describe your friends and enemies, your acquaintances and colleagues—perhaps yourself on occasion?

These words are valuable. Watch for them in your reading; listen for them in your conversation. Use them yourself in your speech and writing— you will be delighted to discover how compactly and forcefully they express precisely what you want to say.

X	X	X	X	X	X	X
X	X	X	X	12	13	14
15	16	17	18	19	20	21
22	23	24	25	26	27	28
29	30					

Words for
Phobias and Manias

We touched on a number of normal human characteristics in the last chapter. Now we turn to a few of the abnormalities of the human mind, to the words that particularize mental peculiarities, neuroses, phobias, and mild or violent personality disorders.

I

Let us discuss, first, five of the most common manias: *kleptomania, pyromania, dipsomania, megalomania,* and *monomania.*

1. The *pyromaniac* (py´-rō-MAY´-nee-ak) has a strange and morbid passion for fire. He will burn down a house with no slightest sense of malice, but merely because he is fascinated by the flames.

2. The *dipsomaniac* (dip´-sō-MAY´-nee-ak) has an uncontrollable compulsion to drink. His vice is a good deal more than a socially pleasant habit, of course. It is an emotional problem, and he must drink and get drunk whether he really wants to or not.

3. The *megalomaniac* (meg-ə-lō-MAY´-nee-ak) has a conviction that he is Napoleon or Caesar, that he has enormous wealth, or even,

sometimes, that he is God. He is continually obsessed by delusions of grandeur.

4. The *monomaniac* (mon´-ō-MAY´-nee-ak) is unbalanced in just one area; on everything else except his own pet and particular delusion he may be completely normal.

5. The *kleptomaniac* (klep´-tō-MAY´-nee-ak) has a compulsion to steal. The victim of this aberration may be wealthy, and the object stolen may be worthless; moreover, the kleptomaniac never has any use for the lifted trinkets, nor any plans for their disposal. He just can't help taking them.

II

Write in the blank lines the word described by each of the following sentences:

1. He can't take one drink and then stop. _____
2. He is mentally deranged on one subject. _____
3. She is apt to steal any little object that she sees. _____
4. He imagines he is God. _____
5. It is dangerous to leave him alone with matches. _____

ANSWERS: (1) dipsomaniac; (2) monomaniac; (3) kleptomaniac; (4) megalomaniac; (5) pyromaniac

III

What's your pet phobia? You haven't any? Don't be too sure. How about your startled-turtle habit of ducking under the bedclothes when the lightning crackles? Or your shudders when a snake crosses your path? Or possibly you edge away from the tops of tall buildings because height makes you feel funny?

If you are an average man you have, not one, but 2.21 phobias.

If you are an average woman you have 3.55 phobias.

Here is a list of the twelve most common phobias. You need not try to remember them, as they will hardly ever be useful to you unless you are a psychiatrist, in which case you already know them.

ceraunophobia	morbid dread of thunder
astraphobia	morbid dread of lightning
ophidiophobia	morbid dread of snakes
nyctophobia	morbid dread of darkness
acrophobia	morbid dread of heights
pyrophobia	morbid dread of fire
aquaphobia	morbid dread of water
ailurophobia	morbid dread of cats
cynophobia	morbid dread of dogs
agoraphobia	morbid dread of open spaces
claustrophobia	morbid dread of close spaces
triskaidekaphobia	morbid dread of the number thirteen

Three of these phobias are particularly common:

1. *Claustrophobia* (klawss´-trə-FŌ-bee-ə). The victim feels choked by small rooms or crowded or confined places. If there is not plenty of open space around him, his discomfort is acute; he may even go into a panic.

2. *Agoraphobia* (ag´-ə-rə-FO´-bee-ə). Contrarily, someone suffering from this problem cannot stand open spaces—very large rooms, public areas that have few people (empty theaters, for example), etc. He finds it painful, if not impossible, to walk across a deserted ball field. He is terrified, in short, by limitless horizons.

3. *Acrophobia* (ak´-rə-FŌ´-bee-ə). The person burdened with this fear is panic-stricken by heights. He cannot mount higher than the third or fourth step of a ladder, cannot look out of the top windows of a tall building, is terrified of rapidly ascending elevators, would rather die than take a plane trip.

IV

Four more people with emotional or mental problems:

1. The *hypochondriac* (hy´-pō-KON´-dree-ak) continually complains about imaginary ills. A heart flutter means heart failure. A headache is a brain tumor. An upset stomach indicates gastric ulcers or cancer. The only real problem is, of course, a morbid imagination.

The ailment: *hypochondria* (hy´-pō-KON´-dree-ə)

2. The *amnesiac* (am-NEE´-zee-ak) suffers from loss of memory. The cause is often a blow on the head or some sudden emotional shock, after which the victim's past becomes a complete blank. He cannot even recognize his family and closest friends. In time, with treatment, there is usually a recovery.

The ailment: *amnesia* (am-NEE´-zhə)

3. The *somnambulist* (səm-NAM´-byə-list) walks in his sleep.

The ailment: *somnambulism* (səm-NAM´-byə-liz-əm)

4. The *insomniac* (in-SOM´-nee-ak) is habitually afflicted with wakefulness at times when he wishes to sleep.

The ailment: *insomnia* (in-SOM´-nee-ə)

V

Who would be most likely to say the following?

1. "What a night. I didn't sleep a wink!" _____
2. "I walked around the room last night? Why, I was fast asleep." _____
3. "Who am I? I've completely forgotten my name." _____
4. "I don't care what the doctor says. I know I've got heart trouble." _____
5. "I can't live in an apartment on the fifth floor. Isn't there anything vacant lower down?" _____
6. "I'm getting out of here. This place is so small I think the walls are going to crush me!" _____

7. "No, thanks, I can't go fishing with you on that
    enormous lake. It goes on forever!" _____

ANSWERS: (1) insomniac; (2) somnambulist; (3) amnesiac;
(4) hypochondriac; (5) acrophobe; (6) claustrophobe; (7) agoraphobe

VI

Four victims of very serious mental illness:

1. The *manic-depressive* (man´-ək-də-PRESS´-iv) has alternating
moods of black depression and wild, uncontrollable exaltation or excit-
ability. Changes are unpredictable and come without warning.

The illness: *manic-depression* (man´-ək-də-PRESH´-ən)

2. The *schizophrenic* (skiz´-ə-FREN´-ək) is a split or divided personality. He loses contact with his environment, lives in an unreal
world of his own making, and often imagines he is someone else.

The illness: *schizophrenia* (skiz´-ə-FREEN´-yə)

3. The *melancholiac* (mel´-ən-KŌ´-lee-ak) has fallen into a fixed
condition of despondency. He often thinks of, or attempts, suicide.

The illness: *melancholia* (mel´-ən-KŌ´-lee-ə)

4. The *paranoiac* (pair´-ə-NOY´-ak) has delusions of persecution.
He imagines that people are trying to poison him, that he is being pur-
sued by enemies, that everyone is against him.

The illness: *paranoia* (pair´-ə-NOY´-ə)

VII

According to Freudian psychology, the person who has grown up without successfully adjusting to the parent-child relationship or to his own
place in the family constellation may develop either of the following:

1. An *Oedipus* (ED´-ə-pəs) *complex.* The male so burdened is the
typical "mama's boy" who has been overprotected and overbabied and
prevented from maturing emotionally. Unconsciously, according to
the Freudians, he has a repressed desire to kill his father and marry his
mother.

2. An *Electra* (ə-LEK´-trə) *complex.* This is the female version of the Oedipal problem—the girl is hostile to her mother, in love with her father.

VIII

Can you match the problem area with the name of the disturbance?

DISTURBANCE	PROBLEM AREA
1. *pyromania*	a. grandeur
2. *dipsomania*	b. illness
3. *megalomania*	c. sleepwalking
4. *monomania*	d. one single obsession
5. *kleptomania*	e. hilarity followed by gloom
6. *hypochondria*	f. fire
7. *amnesia*	g. no contact with reality
8. *somnambulism*	h. persecution
9. *insomniac*	i. attachment to mother
10. *manic-depression*	j. thievery
11. *schizophrenia*	k. open areas
12. *melancholia*	l. high places
13. *paranoia*	m. confined areas
14. *Oedipus complex*	n. memory
15. *Electra complex*	o. liquor
16. *claustrophobia*	p. attachment to father
17. *agoraphobia*	q. overwhelming sadness
18. *acrophobia*	r. sleeplessness

ANSWERS: (1) f; (2) o; (3) a; (4) d; (5) j; (6) b; (7) n; (8) c; (9) r; (10) e; (11) g; (12) q; (13) h; (14) i; (15) p; (16) m; (17) k; (18) l

IX

Write the word that fits each definition. Initial letters are offered to prod your memory.

1. M _____ Continued gloom and depression

2. M _____ Moods of violent excitement alternating with black depression

3. A _____ Loss of memory

4. S _____ Walking and performing other actions during sleep

5. D _____ Uncontrollable craving for alcoholic liquor

6. H _____ Morbid anxiety about one's health

7. P _____ Delusions of persecution

8. E _____ Early and abnormal attachment of a girl for her father, with hostility to her mother

9. K _____ Uncontrollable propensity to steal articles of little value

10. M _____ Delusions of grandeur

11. I _____ Chronic inability to fall asleep

12. M _____ Obsession in a single area

13. P _____ Uncontrollable need to set fires

14. S _____ Mental derangement characterized by loss of contact with reality; split personality

15. C _____ Morbid dread of confined places

16. A _____ Morbid dread of open spaces

17. O _____ Unresolved attachment to mother with accompanying hatred of father

18. A _____ Morbid dread of heights

ANSWERS: (1) melancholia; (2) manic-depression; (3) amnesia;
(4) somnambulism; (5) dipsomania; (6) hypochondria; (7) paranoia;
(8) Electra complex; (9) kleptomania; (10) megalomania;
(11) insomnia; (12) monomania; (13) pyromania; (14) schizophrenia;
(15) claustrophobia; (16) agoraphobia; (17) Oedipus complex;
(18) acrophobia

After such a chapter as this, you may think that we are advocating the use of long and difficult words. But the words we have discussed here are the only ones that accurately describe the troubles and disorders that afflict many people. There are no substitutes for most of them.

But let this rule generally hold. Never, or at least almost never, use a long word where a short one will do. Words, as you well know, are to express your thoughts, not to conceal them. The greatest poems and the greatest speeches, whether it is Robert Burns's "My love is like a red, red rose" or Patrick Henry's "Give me liberty or give me death" all have the power and charm of simplicity. Try to avoid the too frequent use of such Latin words as *juxtaposition, animadvert, salutation, recapitulate*. They tend to make your style heavy, dry, and pedantic. Short Anglo-Saxon words have force—*gift* instead of *donation; poor* instead of *impecunious*. There is a simple beauty in *ship, shop, walk, free, earth, mate, man, friend*. The Latin and Greek words are important to know, but should be used with discretion, and never to overwhelm a reader or listener.

Simplicity and directness in language are always effective.

X	X	X	X	X	X	X
X	X	X	X	X	13	14
15	16	17	18	19	20	21
22	23	24	25	26	27	28
29	30					

Words About Your Feelings

During the last few chapters we have been dealing with all kinds of people—with their peculiarities, their mental quirks, their philosophies, their ideas. Now let us deal with ideas alone. Or shall we get more personal, and consider the terms that describe *your* thoughts, *your* feelings, *your* attitudes and emotions?

Consider these five words:

nostalgia (nos-TAL´-jə)

satiated (SAY´-shee-ay´-təd)

benevolence (bə-NEV´-ə-lənce)

frustration (frus-TRAY´-shən)

lethargy (LETH´-ər-jee)

I

Are any of these strange to you? Consider them in sentences that give a hint to their meanings:

1. He was overcome with a wave of *nostalgia* whenever he thought of his boyhood years in Scotland.
2. The huge dinner left him *satiated*.
3. That morning he was at peace with the world; his attitude toward all mankind was one of *benevolence*.
4. All life, he claims, is *frustration*. The gods seem bent on mischievously thwarting his hopes and plans.
5. His illness left him in a state of *lethargy*; all ambition, interest, desire, were gone.

II

Take the italicized words in Section I and write each one next to its definition.

1. _____ State of apathy or indifference
2. _____ Severe homesickness; a longing for the pleasant past
3. _____ Desire for the welfare of others; charitableness
4. _____ Filled beyond natural desire; glutted
5. _____ Failure or inability to attain something desired

ANSWERS: (1) lethargy; (2) nostalgia; (3) benevolence; (4) satiated; (5) frustration

III

Five more words will now be treated in the same way. Again, try to figure out their meanings from the context of the sentences in which they appear.

enervated (EN´-ər-vay´-təd)
weltschmerz (VELT´-shmairtz)
ennui (AHN´-wee)

compunction (kəm-PUNK´-shən)
antipathy (an-TIP´-ə-thee)

1. His all-night vigil completely *enervated* him.
2. Adolescents are often rather pessimistic about the future of humanity. This *weltschmerz* is a natural result of their maturing minds and bodies.
3. Never had her life been so stagnant and empty. Never had she been so filled with *ennui.*
4. He had no *compunctions* about cheating his peer.
5. He had a violent *antipathy* to all political theories smacking, however faintly, of communism.

IV

Can you pair off each of our new words with its definition below?

1. _____ Literally, world pain; sadness from a gloomy world philosophy
2. _____ An instinctive feeling of aversion or dislike
3. _____ Self-reproach for wrongdoing; slight regret
4. _____ Deprived of physical, nervous, and emotional energy
5. _____ A feeling of listless weariness resulting from satiety, boredom, or inactivity

ANSWERS: (1) weltschmerz; (2) antipathy; (3) compunction; (4) enervated; (5) ennui

V

Here is a third group for study in the same way.

supercilious (soo-pər-SIL´-ee-əs)
vindictive (vin-DIK´-tiv)
misogynist (mə-SAHJ´-ə-nist)
misanthrope (MISS´-ən-thrōp)
vicariously (vy-KAIR´-ee-əs-lee)

1. You are too *supercilious;* what makes you think you're so superior?
2. Be careful not to hurt her feelings, for she'll never forgive you. You know how *vindictive* some people are.
3. Protesters voiced their opposition to explicitly *misogynist* company policies such as paying female employees less than their male counterparts.
4. At heart, he's a *misanthrope.* No wonder he has no friends.
5. Since his accident he has been unable to take part in the sports that he used to love. Now he reads the sports page and enjoys tennis, golf, and baseball *vicariously.*

VI

Again, match each word to its definition.

1. _____ Manner of experiencing something indirectly instead of directly
2. _____ A hater of mankind
3. _____ A hater of women
4. _____ Disposed to revenge; retaliatory
5. _____ Lofty with pride; haughtily contemptuous

ANSWERS: (1) vicariously; (2) misanthrope; (3) misogynist; (4) vindictive; (5) supercilious

VII

Now let's try a reinforcing exercise with all fifteen words. Check your response to each question.

1. When you have a feeling of *lethargy,* are you full of bounce, pep, and ambition? Yes____ No____
2. Is *nostalgia* a yearning for the past? Yes____ No____
3. Do kindly people often feel *benevolent?* Yes____ No____

4. When you haven't eaten for a long time, do you feel *satiated*? Yes____ No____

5. Is *frustration* an unpleasant feeling? Yes____ No____

6. Do pessimistic people often experience *weltschmerz*? Yes____ No____

7. Do you feel *antipathy* to people you like? Yes____ No____

8. Does a cruel and insensitive person have any *compunction* about mistreating others? Yes____ No____

9. Is it normal to wake up *enervated* after a good night's sleep? Yes____ No____

10. If nothing seems exciting or worthwhile, is it justifiable to experience *ennui*? Yes____ No____

11. Is living *vicariously* less fulfilling than direct experience? Yes____ No____

12. Does a *misanthrope* hate everyone? Yes____ No____

13. Does a *misogynist* enjoy the company of females? Yes____ No____

14. Does a *vindictive* person forgive easily? Yes____ No____

15. Does a *supercilious* person usually feel superior to others? Yes____ No____

ANSWERS: (1) No; (2) Yes; (3) Yes; (4) No; (5) Yes; (6) Yes; (7) No; (8) No; (9) No; (10) Yes; (11) Yes; (12) Yes; (13) No; (14) No; (15) Yes

VIII

Ready for more reinforcement? Write S if a pair of words are essentially the *same* in meaning, O if they are more or less *opposed*.

1. *lethargy* ____ energy

2. *nostalgia* ____ homesickness

3. *benevolence* ____ ill will

4. *satiated* ____ full

5. *frustration* ____ satisfaction

6. *weltschmerz* ____ happiness
7. *antipathy* ____ affection
8. *compunctions* ____ scruples
9. *enervated* ____ tired
10. *ennui* ____ boredom
11. *vicariously* ____ actually
12. *misanthrope* ____ philanthropist
13. *misogynist* ____ Don Juan
14. *vindictive* ____ forgiving
15. *supercilious* ____ humble

ANSWERS: (1) o; (2) s; (3) o; (4) s; (5) o; (6) o; (7) o; (8) s; (9) s; (10) s; (11) o; (12) o; (13) o; (14) o; (15) o

IX

A very useful exercise, one that helps you use words in a variety of ways, requires you to experiment with different parts of speech—noun, adjective, adverb, verb. Can you make the proper changes asked for below? An illustrative phrase or sentence and, where possible, an analogy are offered to help you.

1. Change *lethargy* to an adjective to fit into the following phrase: A _____ attitude.
   (*neuralgia—neuralgic*)

2. *Nostalgia* to an adjective: A _____ feeling.
   (*claustrophobia—claustrophobic*)

3. *Benevolence* to an adverb: He beamed _____.
   (*impotence—impotently*)

4. *Satiated* to a negative adjective ending in *-ble:* He is an _____ reader.
   (*estimated—inestimable*)

5. *Satiated* to a noun ending in *-ty:* I've had a _____ of motion pictures.
   (*anxious—anxiety*)

6. *Frustration* to a verb: Why do you try to _____ me?
(*appreciation—appreciate*)

7. *Antipathy* to an adjective: I am _____ to such ideas.
(*sympathy—sympathetic*)

8. *Enervated* to a noun: The cause of his _____.
(*saturated—saturation*)

9. *Vicariously* to an adjective: A _____ thrill.
(*famously—famous*)

10. *Misanthrope* to another noun denoting the person: He is a

_____,

(ends in -*ist*)

11. *Misanthrope* to a noun denoting the philosophy: What is the
cause of his _____?
(*philanthropist—philanthropy*)

12. *Misogynist* to a noun denoting the philosophy: What is the
cause of his _____?
(*botanist—botany*)

13. *Vindictive* to a noun: I dislike him mainly for his _____,
(*active—activeness*)

14. *Supercilious* to a noun: Your _____ will make you lose
many friends.
(*fastidious—fastidiousness*)

ANSWERS: (1) lethargic (lə-THAHR´-jik); (2) nostalgic (nə-STAL´-
jik; (3) benevolently (bə-NEV´-ə-lənt-lee); (4) insatiable (in-SAY´-
shee-ə-bəl); (5) satiety (sə-TY´-ə-tee); (6) frustrate (FRUSS´-trate);
(7) antipathetic (an´-tee-pə-THET´-ik); (8) enervation (ən´-ər-VAY´-
shən); (9) vicarious (vy-KAIR´-ee-əs); (10) misanthropist (mə-SAN´-
thrə-pist); (11) misanthropy (mə-SAN´-thrə-pee); (12) misogyny
(mə-SAHJ´-ə-nee); (13) vindictiveness (vin-DIK´-tiv-nəss);
(14) superciliousness (soo-pər-SIL´-ee-əs-nəss)

X

Now let's sock it home. If all your work with, and exposure to, the words in this chapter have finally made you master of them, you will be able, without doubt or hesitation, to match the *statement of feeling* to each noun below.

NOUNS	STATEMENT OF FEELING
1. *lethargy*	a. "I can't do it!"
2. *nostalgia*	b. "You do it, I'll watch."
3. *benevolence*	c. "All is boredom."
4. *satiety*	d. "I hate everyone!"
5. *frustration*	e. "I'm exhausted, worn out."
6. *weltschmerz*	f. "I hate women!"
7. *antipathy*	g. "I wish I were home."
8. *compunction*	h. "I can't stand it!"
9. *ennui*	i. "I'll get even!"
10. *enervation*	j. "I can't move, can't respond."
11. *vicariousness*	k. "You're dirt!"
12. *misanthropy*	l. "The world is a sad place."
13. *misogyny*	m. "No more, please."
14. *vindictiveness*	n. "I'd better not."
15. *superciliousness*	o. "I wish the best for you."

ANSWERS: (1) j; (2) g; (3) o; (4) m; (5) a; (6) l; (7) h; (8) n; (9) c; (10) e; (11) b; (12) d; (13) f; (14) i; (15) k

Compactly, richly, effectively—and as no others can—these words express deep, living, glowing ideas. Without them you might have to fumble to express what you mean.

Once you know the *exact* word, your ideas come across in simple and immediately understandable clarity.

With a well-stocked arsenal of words at your command, you can become a more powerful, more influential thinker, writer, and speaker.

X	X	X	X	X	X	X
X	X	X	X	X	X	14
15	16	17	18	19	20	21
22	23	24	25	26	27	28
29	30					

Words That End
in "Ology"

Traveling at the rate of 186,000 miles a second, a ray of light started toward the earth with the message that a star had exploded somewhere in space. Thirteen centuries passed by before it arrived. Goethe, Shakespeare, Galileo, and King Arthur's Court all came and went. Napoleon strode over Europe like a colossus, lost his kingdom, and died. America was discovered. Great wars began and ceased and began again while this glimmer of light was racing on to tell our astronomers of a world-shaking catastrophe that had happened in the constellation of Hercules.

This message was read and understood. And that is the triumph of the mind of man.

His intellect can weigh the sun and measure the heat from the farthest star. His eyes can see a billion miles into space and they can also explore the infinitesimal world of electrons. Man has struggled for his knowledge of medicine and archaeology and geology and the multitude of sciences. We, by the miracle of words, can open some of these doors, and if they are so much as barely open, we may be tempted to walk in.

I
THE FIELDS OF HUMAN KNOWLEDGE

1. *Anthropology* (an´-thrō-POL´-ə-jee). This word we have had before and you will recognize it as "the science of mankind" in general, his habits, history, distribution, culture.

2. *Geology* (jee-OL´-ə-jee). The meaning of this word is crystal clear when we know that the "geo" comes from the Greek *geos*, "earth," plus *logos*, "study" or "science." *Geology*, then, is the science of the structure, forces, and history of that whirling planet we call earth.

3. *Archaeology* (ahr´-kee-OL´-ə-jee). This is the science of antiquities. It deals with the old records that man leaves in such forms as buildings and pottery and in the physical remains of his industries. The key to the language of the Aztecs of ancient Mexico, for example, has not been fully discovered, but *archaeologists* can learn much of the story of these people from the ruins they left. (Greek *archaios*, "ancient," and therefore "the study of ancient things.")

4. *Embryology* (em´-bree-OL´-ə-jee). In the early stages of prenatal development, the unborn child is called an *embryo*. Once more the Greeks have helped us, for *en* in their language means "in," and *bryein*, "swell"; so, literally, the word means "to swell inside," which is just what happens in pregnancy. An *embryologist*, then, deals with the beginnings of life.

5. *Entomology* (en´-tə-MOL´-ə-jee). When you know that *entomon* is Greek for "insect," the rest is easy to guess. The *entomologists* have given us a wealth of knowledge about the home life, sex habits, and social customs of bees, ants, butterflies, and other members of the species.

6. *Ethnology* (eth-NOL´-ə-jee). People with different traits and qualities around the world. What is their history? Where did they come from? Where do they live? How do they differ in mind, culture, characteristics? These are questions for the *ethnologist* to answer. From Greek, *ethnos*, "race."

7. *Etymology* (et´-ə-MOL´-ə-jee). You will recall that this is the study of the history and origin of words.

8. *Ornithology* (awr´-nə-THOL´-ə-jee). If you are told that *ornis* is Greek for "bird," you can find your own meaning. The lives and habits of eagles and whippoorwills, tanagers and sparrows, hawks and seagulls—all such are the province of the *ornithologist*.

9. *Philology* (fə-LOL´-ə-jee). This word we are already familiar with. The *philologist* covers the entire field of words and language, the whole area of linguistics.

10. *Psychology* (sy-KOL´-ə-jee). Once more let's leaf over the pages of our Greek lexicon, and we find *psyche*, "soul," "mind." So the *psychologist* is a student of, and an authority on, the human mind, and human behavior in all of its aspects.

II
REVIEW YOUR LEARNING

Here are the ten fields of human knowledge once again, in simple chart form, with the scientist in parentheses next to each one. Can you review in your mind the area of interest of each scientist in preparation for a reinforcing test?

THE FIELD	THE AREA
1. *anthropology* (*anthropologist*)	_____
2. *geology* (*geologist*)	_____
3. *archaeology* (*archaeologist*)	_____
4. *embryology* (*embryologist*)	_____
5. *entomology* (*entomologist*)	_____
6. *ethnology* (*ethnologist*)	_____
7. *etymology* (*etymologist*)	_____
8. *ornithology* (*ornithologist*)	_____
9. *philology* (*philologist*)	_____
10. *psychology* (*psychologist*)	_____

III
WHERE DOES ONE TURN?

If you wished the answer to each of the following questions, to which of the specialists in Section II would you turn for your information?

1. What does the unborn baby look like during the third week of its development? _____

2. How many Mayan ruins are there in Central America? _____

3. What makes human beings behave the way they do? _____

4. What kind of rock is found in Tennessee? _____

5. Is it true that the owl is wiser than other birds? _____

6. What did the men of the Stone Age look like? _____

7. What is the life span of an ant? _____

8. What is the derivation or origin of the word *boycott*? _____

9. How many different languages are spoken in Europe? _____

10. What traits and qualities do all people share in common? _____

ANSWERS: (1) embryologist; (2) archaeologist; (3) psychologist; (4) geologist; (5) ornithologist; (6) anthropologist; (7) entomologist; (8) etymologist; (9) philologist; (10) ethnologist

IV
DON'T STOP NOW!

There are still many things you can do with these words. Say them aloud, many times. That is the first step toward making them your own. If you aren't perfectly comfortable with their pronunciation, you won't dare to use them.

Try spelling them. Get a friend or a member of your family to help you by dictating the words while you write them. Each step is a clincher that helps hold the words more firmly in your mind, helps you feel more at home with them.

Experiment with the etymologies. The Greek *geos* means "earth." How easy it is then to read the meaning of *geography, geopolitics, geometry.*

Anthropos is "mankind"; thus *misanthropy, philanthropy,* and *anthropoid* (similar to man) fall right in place.

Archaios, "ancient," gives us *archaic* (ancient, no longer used, old-fashioned), and *archetype* (the ancient, or original, model), as well as *archaeology.*

Psyche, "soul" or "mind," produces words like *psychic, psychiatry, psychoanalysis, psychotic,* as well as *psychology.* Once you recognize the root, the word itself can no longer be a complete mystery to you.

The *philologist* loves words—from *philein,* "to love," and *logos,* one of whose meanings is "word" (the other is "study of"). *Philadelphia* is the City of Brotherly Love; a *philatelist* loves stamps; a *bibliophile* loves books; a *philanthropist* loves mankind; a *philosopher* loves wisdom; a *philtre* is a love potion. We repeat: Know the root, and the word is no longer a mystery.

So let's end the chapter by giving you a chance to fix the roots and meanings in your mind. Can you match the two columns below?

1.	*anthropos* (*anthropology*)	a. earth
2.	*archaios* (*archaeology*)	b. race
3.	*geos* (*geology*)	c. insect
4.	*bryein* (*embryology*)	d. bird
5.	*entomon* (*entomology*)	e. mind, soul
6.	*ethnos* (*ethnology*)	f. mankind
7.	*ornis* (*ornithology*)	g. word, study of
8.	*philein* (*philology*)	h. to love
9.	*psyche* (*psychology*)	i. to swell
10.	*logos* (*etymology*)	j. ancient

ANSWERS: (1) f; (2) j; (3) a; (4) i; (5) c; (6) b; (7) d; (8) h; (9) e; (10) g

✗	✗	✗	✗	✗	✗	✗
✗	✗	✗	✗	✗	✗	✗
15	16	17	18	19	20	21
22	23	24	25	26	27	28
29	30					

Words for Human Traits

Men and women have so many forms of behavior, and such a multitude of varied characteristics and points of view, that they have inspired a host of descriptive adjectives. We will introduce the new words first in a series of simple sentences to give at least a hint to their meanings.

I

1. The *loquacious* (lō-KWAY´-shəs) person talks incessantly.
2. The *gullible* (GULL´-ə-bəl) person believes everything a canvasser tells them.
3. The *suave* (SWAHV) talker can persuade you that black is white.
4. The *pompous* (POM´-pəs) person seems overwhelmed with a sense of his own importance.
5. The *esthetic* (es-THET´-ik) artist has dedicated his life to beauty.

6. The *taciturn* (TAS´-ə-turn) husband answers his wife in grunts and monosyllables, if at all.

7. The *opinionated* (ə-PIN´-yə-nay´-təd) fool has a mind so finally made up that neither hell nor high water can make him change it.

8. The *phlegmatic* (fleg-MAT´-ik) person can't get excited over anything.

9. The *erudite* (AIR´-ə-dite) man is full of book learning.

10. The *complacent* (kəm-PLAY´-sənt) fellow is sure that everything is going to come out all right.

11. The *punctilious* (punk-TILL´-ee-əs) hostess worries if so much as one fork is out of place on her perfectly set table.

12. The *indefatigable* (in´-de-FAT´-ə-gə-bəl) worker seems capable of getting along on four hours' sleep a day.

13. The *vapid* (VAP´-id) talker's conversation is completely boring.

14. The *iconoclastic* (eye-kon´-ə-KLASS´-tik) critic carps at such institutions as government, marriage, and religion.

15. The *misanthropic* (miss´-ən-THROP´-ik) cynic hates the world and everybody in it.

16. The *puerile* (PYOO´-ər-əl) practical joker may have grown up physically, but is still a child emotionally.

17. The *ascetic* (a-SET´-ik) person lives in a hut and likes it.

II

These words have been used in sentences that aim at giving you enough of a clue to spark your interest in figuring out the possible meanings. How successfully can you find the italicized word in Section I that best fits each of the following definitions?

1. Completely self-satisfied; smug _____

2. Smooth and pleasant in manner; bland; gracious; smoothly ingratiating _____

3. By temperament, not easily perturbed; calm; emotionally sluggish or unresponsive _____

4. One who assails or mocks traditional or cherished beliefs _____

5. Simple; credulous; easily deceived _____

6. Marked by assumed self-importance; pretentious _____

7. Appreciating or loving the beautiful; artistic _____

8. Characteristic of childhood; juvenile; immature and silly or trivial _____

9. Very learned; scholarly _____

10. Practicing extreme abstinence; austere and rigorous in self-denial or self-discipline _____

11. Extremely talkative _____

12. Habitually silent or unwilling to engage in conversation _____

13. Unduly attached to one's own opinions; obstinate in holding on to beliefs _____

14. Not exhausted by labor or exercise; never tiring _____

15. Hating mankind _____

16. Very exact or scrupulous in the observance of forms of etiquette, ceremony, or behavior _____

17. Utterly lacking in sparkle, flavor, or interest; empty and flat _____

ANSWERS: (1) complacent; (2) suave; (3) phlegmatic; (4) iconoclastic; (5) gullible; (6) pompous; (7) esthetic; (8) puerile; (9) erudite; (10) ascetic; (11) loquacious; (12) taciturn; (13) opinionated; (14) indefatigable; (15) misanthropic; (16) punctilious; (17) vapid

III

Our theory throughout this book, as you have no doubt already observed, is that the best way to learn new words effectively is the way that everyone, from infancy on, learns them—namely, by gradual, step-by-step increasing of understanding. It is the repeated contact with a word in many different contexts that finally makes you so familiar and comfortable with it that you eventually feel it was always in your vocabulary. It is at this point that you begin using the word in your thinking, speaking, and writing—and you do so unself-consciously, without effort, and so unexpectedly that sometimes you even surprise yourself.

You have now had two exposures to the seventeen words that make up this chapter—once in a sentence, once in matching them to their definitions. Here is your third exposure: a series of phrases, each of which should produce a flash of recognition in you that helps you react with one of the seventeen words. Do not look back as you do this exercise—the initial letter of the word is a sufficient prod to your power to recall. Several of the adjectives will be required more than once.

In this exercise you should begin to feel the first surges of power and self-confidence as you zip through, writing each word as it is called for.

1. Emotionally sluggish   P_____
2. Practicing self-denial   A_____
3. Disinclined to conversation   T_____
4. Having an antipathy for mankind   M_____
5. Easily duped   G_____
6. Insipid   V_____
7. Scholarly   E_____
8. Talkative   L_____
9. Precise in the observance of forms   P_____
10. Ostentatiously self-important   P_____
11. Inane   V_____

12. Responsive to beauty   E _____
13. Descriptive of the attitude of one who attacks cherished beliefs as shams   I _____
14. Childish   P _____
15. Polished in manner   S _____
16. Stubbornly set in opinions   O _____
17. Self-satisfied   C _____
18. Attacking established traditions   I _____
19. Having an aversion for the human race   M _____
20. Tireless   I _____
21. Urbanely smooth and ingratiating   S _____
22. Contented with oneself and with things as they are
    C _____

ANSWERS: (1) phlegmatic; (2) ascetic; (3) taciturn; (4) misanthropic; (5) gullible; (6) vapid; (7) erudite; (8) loquacious; (9) punctilious; (10) pompous; (11) vapid; (12) esthetic; (13) iconoclastic; (14) puerile; (15) suave; (16) opinionated; (17) complacent; (18) iconoclasm; (19) misanthropic; (20) indefatigable; (21) suave; (22) complacent

IV

Now test your increasing understanding of these seventeen words by marking each of the following statements "true" or "false":

1. Talkative people are called *loquacious*.
   True_____ False_____
2. Clumsy drunks are as a rule *suave*.
   True_____ False_____
3. The stereotype of the truck driver is usually *esthetic*.
   True_____ False_____
4. Enthusiastic people are usually *taciturn*.
   True_____ False_____

5. The more impartial a man is, the more *opinionated* he
   sounds.
   True____ False____

6. *Phlegmatic* people usually become panicky in an emergency.
   True____ False____

7. *Pomposity* is usually amusing.
   True____ False____

8. College professors are often *erudite*.
   True____ False____

9. Smug people are never *complacent*.
   True____ False____

10. *Punctilious* people are sticklers for form.
    True____ False____

11. The beaver is an *indefatigable* worker.
    True____ False____

12. The conversation of a conceited bore is usually *vapid*.
    True____ False____

13. The attitude of young people is usually *iconoclastic*.
    True____ False____

14. *Misanthropic* remarks show a feeling of love and trust
    for people.
    True____ False____

15. *Puerile* behavior indicates maturity.
    True____ False____

16. An *ascetic* existence is given over to sensuality.
    True____ False____

17. A young child is apt to be *gullible*.
    True____ False____

ANSWERS: (1) true; (2) false; (3) false; (4) false; (5) false; (6) false;
(7) true; (8) true; (9) false; (10) true; (11) true; (12) true; (13) true;
(14) false; (15) false; (16) false; (17) true

V

Continuing your gradual reinforcement of understanding through stimulus and response, try a different type of test. Check the word or phrase that best completes each sentence.

1. *Loquacity* is an inordinate amount of:
   a. singing
   b. attention to details
   c. talking

2. *Gullible* people fall easy prey to:
   a. doctors
   b. con artists
   c. teachers

3. *Suave* men are experts at:
   a. home repair
   b. surfing
   c. getting along with women

4. *Pomposity* probably comes from:
   a. fear
   b. obesity
   c. vanity

5. Most likely to be *esthetic* is an:
   a. electrician
   b. aviator
   c. artist

6. *Taciturnity* would likely be found in:
   a. salesmen
   b. public speakers
   c. hermits

7. *Opinionated* assertions may likely lead to:
   a. marriage

    b.   arguments

    c.   truth

8. A *phlegmatic* person:

    a.   sheds tears at an emotional play

    b.   becomes hysterical in a crisis

    c.   does not become easily emotional

9. *Erudite* men are most interested in:

    a.   scholarly books

    b.   light fiction

    c.   the comics

10. People who are *complacent* about their jobs will:

    a.   take it easy

    b.   worry about their future

    c.   keep an eye on the help-wanted ads

11. A *punctilious* person is a stickler for:

    a.   originality

    b.   courage

    c.   proper etiquette

12. To be *indefatigable,* one usually needs a great amount of:

    a.   money

    b.   energy

    c.   education

13. *Vapid* people are:

    a.   boring

    b.   successful

    c.   quarrelsome

14. *Iconoclasts* are opposed to:

    a.   change

    b.   tradition

    c.   reform

15. A *misanthrope* dislikes:

    a.   people

    b.   good food

    c.   literature

16.   Men are most likely to be *puerile* when:

    a.   they don't get their own way

    b.   they are reading

    c.   they are eating

17.   Most *ascetics* prefer to:

    a.   drink excessively

    b.   eat sparingly

    c.   participate in orgies

ANSWERS: (1) c; (2) b; (3) c; (4) c; (5) c; (6) c; (7) b; (8) c; (9) a; (10) a; (11) c; (12) b; (13) a; (14) b; (15) a; (16) a; (17) b

VI

Ready for a final, and considerably harder, challenge? Write the adjective we have studied that is essentially *opposed in meaning* to each of the following words or phrases. Do you now feel sufficiently self-confident not to look back at previous pages as you search your mind for the answers?

1.   taciturn _____

2.   easily swayed to change one's mind _____

3.   ignorant _____

4.   philanthropic _____

5.   blind to beauty _____

6.   lazy _____

7.   dissatisfied _____

8.   conservative _____

9.   mature _____

10.   careless of etiquette; informal _____

11.   voluptuous; pleasure-loving _____

12.   boorish _____

13.   modest, humble _____

14. loquacious _____
15. high-strung _____
16. skeptical _____
17. clever and interesting _____

ANSWERS: (1) loquacious; (2) opinionated; (3) erudite;
(4) misanthropic; (5) esthetic; (6) indefatigable; (7) complacent;
(8) iconoclastic; (9) puerile; (10) punctilious; (11) ascetic; (12) suave;
(13) pompous; (14) taciturn; (15) phlegmatic; (16) gullible; (17) vapid

VII

There are interesting etymologies behind many of the words in this chapter.

Suave: Latin *suavis,* "sweet" or "smooth."

Iconoclastic: Greek *eikon,* "idol"; *klaein,* "to break." An *iconoclast,* then, is a breaker of idols, or, in the modern sense, a breaker of traditions.

Pompous: Latin *pompa,* "parade" or "solemn procession."

Esthetic: Greek *aisthetikos,* "perceptive," became refined in our language until it referred to the finer feelings and perceptions in the field of art and culture.

Puerile: Latin *puer,* "boy." When a man is *puerile* he is acting like an ungrown boy.

Ascetic: Greek *asketikos,* "self-denying or self-disciplined for purposes of gymnastic excellence." Eventually, our English word took on a more general, all-inclusive meaning.

Loquacious: Latin *loquor,* "speak." *Eloquent* and *colloquial* come from the same root.

Taciturn: Latin *tacere,* "be silent."

Opinionated: Latin *opinio,* "thought" or "opinion." *Opinionated* came to mean too well provided with opinions, and, finally, stubborn or set in opinions.

Indefatigable: Latin *in,* "not," and *defatigare,* "to tire out."

Punctilious: Latin *punctum,* "point." *Punctilious* is used in our language to refer to someone who is very attentive to fine points. *Punctual* and *puncture* derive from the same root.

Vapid: Latin *vapidus,* "flavorless"—and *vapidus* itself is from Latin *vappa,* a wine that has lost its life or savor.

X	X	X	X	X	X	X
X	X	X	X	X	X	X
X	16	17	18	19	20	21
22	23	24	25	26	27	28
29	30					

Words for Human Faults

Have you ever met the carefree young bachelor whose life seems to be one *peccadillo* after another? Does such a one have to be a man of some wealth, or can he follow his manner of life in the midst of *penury*? Do his successes with the opposite sex tend to give him a touch of *megalomania*? His life is certainly an interesting one: that is, if you consider that one *imbroglio* after another makes for interest. Just listen to him talk. His *braggadocio* may entertain his younger acquaintances, but it certainly becomes tiresome to his older friends.

I

Pronounce each word carefully:

1. *peccadillo* (pek´-ə-DIL´-ō)
2. *penury* (PEN´-yə-ree)
3. *megalomania* (meg´-ə-lə-MAY´-nee-ə)
4. *imbroglio* (im-BRŌ´-lyō)
5. *braggadocio* (brag´-ə-DŌ´-shee-ō)

II

From an analysis of the paragraph above, can you match each word to its definition?

1. A complicated and embarrassing situation _____
2. A slight sin _____
3. Empty boasting _____
4. Abject poverty _____
5. Grandiose delusions of one's own importance _____

ANSWERS: (1) imbroglio; (2) peccadillo; (3) braggadocio; (4) penury; (5) megalomania

III

What kind of person are you? Do you think money is a *panacea*? Do you feel your life has been a *fiasco*? What are some of your *idiosyncrasies*? Do you tend to *rationalize* rather than face the truth? Are there *anomalies* in your life that you would like to see removed? The answers to these questions may reveal a number of interesting things about your character.

IV

1. *panacea* (pan´-ə-SEE´-ə)
2. *fiasco* (fee-ASS´-kō)
3. *idiosyncrasy* (id´-ee-ə-SIN´-krə-see)
4. *rationalize* (RASH´-ə-nə-lize´)
5. *anomaly* (ə-NOM´-ə-lee)

V

1. Something that is irregular or inconsistent _____
2. A cure for all ills _____

3. A miserable and ridiculous failure _____
4. To perceive sense in a discreditable act _____
5. A characteristic peculiarity _____

ANSWERS: (1) anomaly; (2) panacea; (3) fiasco; (4) rationalize; (5) idiosyncrasy

VI

Do you by chance have a neurotic friend who is so lazy that he tends to *malinger*? Or one who belongs to the *élite* and looks down his social nose at the *parvenus*? The conversation of such a person is apt to be *banal*, certainly not as interesting as that of the *intelligentsia*. Or have you ever been up against a politician who resorts to *jingoism* and *chicanery* because he cannot gain his end by honest means?

VII

1. *malinger* (mə-LING´-gər)
2. *élite* (ay´-LEET´)
3. *parvenu* (PAR´-və-noo͞)
4. *jingoism* (JING´-gō-iz-əm)
5. *intelligentsia* (in-tell´-ə-JEN´-see-ə)
6. *chicanery* (shə-KAY´-nə-ree)
7. *banal* (BAY´-nəl)

VIII

1. The best or most capable part of any group _____
2. One who flaunts, somewhat vulgarly, newly attained wealth (used contemptuously) _____
3. To feign sickness to shirk work or duty _____
4. Favoring a warlike foreign policy _____
5. The intelligent and educated classes _____

6. Mean, petty trickery _____

7. Commonplace; without sparkle or originality _____

ANSWERS: (1) élite; (2) parvenu; (3) malinger; (4) jingoism;
(5) intelligentsia; (6) chicanery; (7) banal

IX

You have had your first involvement with seventeen new words. Remember, your aim is to become more and more comfortable with new words by meeting them in different situations, working with them in different ways. So now let's try this: Review the preceding pages of this chapter, pronouncing the seventeen words aloud often enough to feel quite at home with them. Then, without further reference, write each one next to the phrase below that is closest in meaning to it. The initial letter is offered as a guide.

1. Extreme poverty or want   P _____

2. The best   E _____

3. A complete or humiliating failure   F _____

4. Trickery   C _____

5. To feign illness in order to escape work   M _____

6. To find a worthier motive for   R _____

7. A deviation from type; an irregularity   A _____

8. Remedy for all diseases   P _____

9. A bellicose foreign policy   J _____

10. Educated and intellectual people   I _____

11. Ordinary; dull   B _____

12. Delusions of grandeur   M _____

13. Pretentious boasting   B _____

14. A slight or trifling sin   P _____

15. A confused and complicated situation   I _____

16. A characteristic peculiarity   I _____

17. A *nouveau riche*; a newly wealthy person   P _____

ANSWERS: (1) penury; (2) élite; (3) fiasco; (4) chicanery; (5) malinger; (6) rationalize; (7) anomaly; (8) panacea; (9) jingoism; (10) intelligentsia; (11) banal; (12) megalomania; (13) braggadocio; (14) peccadillo; (15) imbroglio; (16) idiosyncrasy; (17) parvenu

X

Here's another exercise for still further reinforcement and continuing success. Check whether each pair below is nearly the *same* or *opposite* in meaning.

1. *peccadillo*   slight sin   Same____ Opposite____
2. *penury*   wealth   Same____ Opposite____
3. *megalomania*   humility   Same____ Opposite____
4. *imbroglio*   confusion   Same____ Opposite____
5. *braggadocio*   boasting   Same____ Opposite____
6. *panacea*   cure-all   Same____ Opposite____
7. *fiasco*   success   Same____ Opposite____
8. *idiosyncrasy*   peculiarity   Same____ Opposite____
9. *rationalize*   justify   Same____ Opposite____
10. *anomaly*   irregularity   Same____ Opposite____
11. *malinger*   pretend illness   Same____ Opposite____
12. *élite*   the worst   Same____ Opposite____
13. *parvenu*   *nouveau riche*   Same____ Opposite____
14. *jingoism*   pacifism   Same____ Opposite____
15. *intelligentsia*   the feeble-minded   Same____ Opposite____
16. *chicanery*   honesty   Same____ Opposite____
17. *banal*   original   Same____ Opposite____

ANSWERS: (1) same; (2) opposite; (3) opposite; (4) same; (5) same; (6) same; (7) opposite; (8) same; (9) same; (10) same; (11) same; (12) opposite; (13) same; (14) opposite; (15) opposite; (16) opposite; (17) opposite

XI

Note how other people have used some of these words:

1. As Professor Owen has remarked, there is no greater *anomaly* in nature than a bird that cannot fly.

    (DARWIN)

2. Owing to the disunion of the Fenians themselves, the rigor of the administration, and the treachery of informers, the (Irish) rebellion was a *fiasco*.

    (*The Encyclopedia Britannica*)

3. *Idiosyncrasies* are, however, frequent; thus we find that one person has an exceptional memory for sounds, another for colors, another for forms.

    (*The Encyclopedia Britannica*)

4. The chemists pretended it was the philosopher's stone, the physicians that it was an infallible *panacea*.

    (WHARTON)

5. The Koran attaches much importance to prayer—a fact which is somewhat *anomalous* in a system of religion so essentially fatalistic.

    (SPENCER)

6. Men who by legal *chicanery* cheat others out of their property.

    (SPENCER)

7. Who doesn't forgive? The virtuous Mrs. Grundy. She remembers her neighbors' *peccadilloes* to the third and fourth generations.

    (THACKERAY)

8. I have always observed through life that it is your *parvenu* who stickles for what he calls the genteel, and has the most squeamish abhorrence for what is frank and natural.

    (THACKERAY)

9. 'Tis low ebb with his accusers when such *peccadilloes* as
these are put in to swell the charge.

(BISHOP OF ATTERBURY)

XII

You are now halfway through this book.

How is your work going? Do you feel you are making progress? Here are a few suggestions that may increase the speed of your achievement.

Try laying out a simple, definite, but not overambitious plan for your daily study, if you haven't already done so. Choosing a fixed time each day for this work will be helpful. But if that should be impractical, then learn the fine art of using your spare moments. John Erskine, the famous author, trained himself to use all those minutes of the day that other people waste, and during these periods of salvaged time he wrote most of his novels.

Above all, make this present study a habit, like getting dressed or undressed, combing your hair or brushing your teeth, so that it will become a part of your life and you will turn to it as naturally as you have breakfast in the morning.

And here is a rule that busy people have found invaluable. Always plan your next day's work the night before.

~~1~~	~~2~~	~~3~~	~~4~~	~~5~~	~~6~~	~~7~~
~~8~~	~~9~~	~~10~~	~~11~~	~~12~~	~~13~~	~~14~~
~~15~~	~~16~~	17	18	19	20	21
22	23	24	25	26	27	28
29	30					

You Help to Create the American Language

We have now come to an interval, a halfway mark, in our consideration of words.

We can take a little time out to discuss the matter of who owns this language that we have been studying.

Well, *you* own it. And you. And you. The English language belongs to you. You made it. You are making it every day. You have invented upward of 600,000 usable English words, minus those that have been taken over from other languages. But even these were adopted by you. You have devised the strange spellings of English words. You have determined their pronunciations.

In English we are dealing with an inexact art, not an exact science. Even the mistakes of English are human. Some of our fantastic spellings in this book that you hold in your hand are due merely to the errors of ignorant typesetters who lived centuries ago. We have merely preserved and honored their misspellings. Pronunciations and meanings are frequently modified with just as little reason.

How then, specifically, do you control the language?

In this way: During this present year about five thousand new words will come into our language. Intense and dramatic times such as these are always prolific in breeding new words. The scholars won't mint or invent these new words. They will just pop up. The scholars will have nothing whatsoever to say about how they shall be pronounced or spelled, or what they shall mean. They will be pronounced and spelled and defined pretty much as the public pleases. If you were to ask the editor of the *Funk & Wagnalls New Standard Dictionary* or of *Webster's* or of the *Oxford English Dictionary* or of any other, "Who decides about these new words?" this editor would answer, "You do," meaning, of course, the many millions of "you" who use our language.

Let's take a case in point. *Television* was invented and one of you thought up the word *telecast* as a parallel term to *broadcast*. Scholars called it a bastard type of word, half from the Greek *tele*, "far away," and half from the English word *cast*, but *telecast* it was just the same, thanks to the common people who included it in the current coin of their conversation.

In similar fashion—that is, by usage—old words completely change their meanings, nice words become coarse, and coarse words become respectable.

Slang, for instance, is a good example of the latter move on the part of words.

A great mass of our language was once the slang of the various gas house districts of the world. A large part of it came from over the railroad tracks. Purists and highbrows protested and fulminated against it, but little by little common usage made many of these words so respectable that the scholars were willing to use them and were forced to include them in the dictionaries.

Around 230 years ago, for example, Dean Swift was kicking (slang) at the then current use of such slang words as *bubble, sham,* and *bully* as "a disgrace to our language." Now you and I use them very happily. Let us recite a few more that were once slang: *gin, boycott, cab, greenhorn, hoax, jingoist.*

You see, the masses kept on using these words until they *had* to be included in our lexicons. And conversely, when these or any other words such as those that are included in this volume stop being commonly used, they will die and drop out of our dictionary. *You* will determine this, and our lexicographers will have nothing to do with it.

Now, by just what methods did such words, for instance, as you have been working with in this book ever get into the dictionary?

This is the way. The technique may be interesting to you.

Somebody writes in and asks the dictionary publisher about an apparently new word, or a staff reader discovers it among the Niagara of words pouring out from the presses of the world. So they first check it to find if it really *is* new. They look for it in all the standard English reference works that have come out during the last two centuries. If they don't find it there, and since it might be foreign, they leaf through glossaries of Sanskrit, Maori, Hansa, Urdu, Hebrew, Afrikaans, and all the languages, ancient and modern, that were spawned by the Tower of Babel. If it still evades them, they take a look at the trade and professional dictionaries—say, those of lace-making, politics, petroleum, draperies, botany, and others too numerous to count.

By this time it's a foxy word that's going to fool them!

If the term proves itself as new, they put it on file for about five years.

Now how does it get in?

They watch its *use* by the people during the probationary period. Authors may take it up. Inquiries may come to the office about its meaning. At the end of the interval the record of the neophyte is added up, and *if its score shows a sufficient popular demand,* the word goes in the dictionary. Thus and no otherwise.

Now, how is it *defined*? To be concrete, how were the definitions of the words in the last chapter originally determined upon?

As the researchers watch a new word in use they copy the actual sentences in which the word appears. When a given dictionary editor finally sits down to make up his definition, he will have in front of him a stack of cards containing sentences that give the word and the context. The meaning, or the meanings, that he gives the word will be based, *not in any way on his own opinion,* but upon the sheaf of popular quotations he finds in front of him. His authority, and the authority of the dictionary, then, lie, not in this editor's particular scholarship, but in *your* whim and in the whim of the other millions who have invented, pronounced, spelled, and defined the word for him.

And so when we study the English language we are studying our own handiwork. It is as democratic as our national institutions, and the so-called "common people" are its inexhaustible source. The final authority for English rests, not with some dictionary House of Lords, but with the House of Commons, and this is what gives our language its vitality, force, and rich humanity, and is what helps to make it such a thrilling study.

~~1~~	~~2~~	~~3~~	~~4~~	~~5~~	~~6~~	~~7~~
~~8~~	~~9~~	~~10~~	~~11~~	~~12~~	~~13~~	~~14~~
~~15~~	~~16~~	~~17~~	18	19	20	21
22	23	24	25	26	27	28
29	30					

A "Pop Quiz"

At this point, we are going to challenge you with a surprise test that will give you a yardstick by which you can measure the success you are having in keeping new words in your mind.

We are going to take a single past chapter and see how successfully you've mastered it.

I

Here are the fifteen words from Chapter XII:

lethargy	*enervated*
nostalgia	*ennui*
benevolence	*vicariously*
satiated	*misanthrope*
frustration	*misogynist*
weltschmerz	*vindictive*
antipathy	*supercilious*
compunction	

II

Write each word next to its synonym or synonymous phrase. Some words may be required more than once.

1. Aversion _____
2. Exhausted _____
3. Indirect or second-hand _____
4. Sluggishness _____
5. Tedium _____
6. Weariness of life; sadness for the world _____
7. Remorseful feeling _____
8. Revengeful _____
9. Dislike _____
10. Deprived of vitality _____
11. Longing for the past _____
12. Woman-hater _____
13. Condescending _____
14. Inability to succeed or achieve _____
15. Philosophical and emotional world-sorrow _____
16. Kindheartedness _____
17. Regret for wrongdoing _____
18. Filled full _____

ANSWERS: (1) antipathy; (2) enervated; (3) vicarious; (4) lethargy; (5) ennui; (6) weltschmerz; (7) compunction; (8) vindictiveness; (9) antipathy; (10) enervated; (11) nostalgia; (12) misogynist; (13) supercilious; (14) frustration; (15) weltschmerz; (16) benevolence; (17) compunction; (18) satiated

III

Some of the following statements are false, others are true. Check the correct response.

1. *Misanthropes* have an *antipathy* toward their fellow men.
   True____ False____

2. Staying up all night is *enervating*.
   True____ False____

3. One can get a *vicarious* thrill from the movies.
   True____ False____

4. People full of energy are usually *lethargic*.
   True____ False____

5. Young girls are filled with *ennui* at their first party.
   True____ False____

6. Optimistic people are weighed down with *weltschmerz*.
   True____ False____

7. A military conqueror has strong *compunctions* about taking other people's land.
   True____ False____

8. *Vindictiveness* is an exceedingly attractive trait.
   True____ False____

9. *Nostalgia* is a prevalent ill among young people who are away from home for the first time.
   True____ False____

10. Haters of women are called *misogynists*.
    True____ False____

11. The intelligent members of motion-picture audiences have had a *satiety* of bad pictures.
    True____ False____

12. The depression generation of the 1930s experienced poignant *frustration*.
    True____ False____

13. Adolf Hitler was famous for his great *benevolence*.
    True____ False____

14. Modest people are *supercilious*.
    True____ False____

ANSWERS: (1) true; (2) true; (3) true; (4) false; (5) false; (6) false; (7) false; (8) false; (9) true; (10) true; (11) true; (12) true; (13) false; (14) false

IV

Here are twelve words and phrases, each one *opposed* in meaning to one of our fifteen words. Can you summon from your mind the word that is *antonymous* to each of the following?

1. Joy in living _____
2. Exhilaration _____
3. Chivalry _____
4. Forgivingness _____
5. Sympathy _____
6. First-hand experience _____
7. Keen interest _____
8. Heartlessness _____
9. Hunger _____
10. Feeling of inferiority _____
11. Success _____
12. Malice _____

ANSWERS: (1) weltschmerz; (2) enervation; (3) misogyny; (4) vindictiveness; (5) antipathy; (6) vicariousness; (7) ennui; (8) compunction; (9) satiety; (10) superciliousness; (11) frustration; (12) benevolence

V

Complete each of the following sentences by one of our fifteen words, or by some form of that word. Not all the words may be required, and some words may be asked for more than once.

1. When I reflect on the pleasant memories of my childhood, I am overcome by a wave of _____.
2. Nothing I do is successful; all, all is _____.

3. I would have too many _____ to deprive him of his one chance of happiness.

4. What is life? What is to be the future of humanity? Shall we all finally destroy one another? I am weighed down with _____.

5. No, I don't care to meet that beautiful actress. You forget that I am _____.

6. No wonder you are bored and blasé. You are suffering from a _____ of pleasure.

7. Oh, I think I shall die if something doesn't happen to relieve my _____.

8. You show your superiority too openly. No wonder your friends dislike you and call you _____.

9. I have been unable to accomplish anything for the past two years. I seem to have sunk into a state of _____.

10. _____ have an _____ for women.

11. You treat your employees with a pretended generosity and _____, but they see through you and know that you actually have an _____ for the working classes.

12. Staying up all night dancing has reduced me to a state of _____.

13. I bear you no grudge for what you have done. I am not _____.

14. I see the motion pictures _____ even though I am blind, for my friends come home and tell me all about them.

ANSWERS: (1) nostalgia; (2) frustration; (3) compunctions; (4) weltschmerz; (5) misogynous *or* misogynistic; (6) satiety; (7) ennui; (8) supercilious; (9) lethargy; (10) misogynists, antipathy; (11) benevolence, antipathy; (12) enervation; (13) vindictive; (14) vicariously

X̶	X̶	X̶	X̶	X̶	X̶	X̶
X̶	X̶	X̶	X̶	X̶	X̶	X̶
X̶	X̶	X̶	X̶	19	20	21
22	23	24	25	26	27	28
29	30					

Words About Personalities

Language, most naturally, is an intensely human subject, and all words lead finally to man.

We will turn to terms that deal directly with your friends and with you. Here are twelve words that describe different kinds of personalities.

I

WHAT KIND OF PERSONALITY DO YOU HAPPEN TO HAVE?

1. Are you reserved, quiet, happy to be alone? Do you spend much of your time thinking of yourself? You are probably an *introvert*.

2. Are you a good mixer? Do you prefer the company of others to solitude? Are you rarely self-conscious and usually more interested in the outside world and in the other fellow than you are in yourself? Would you be apt to make a good salesman? You are probably an *extrovert*.

3. Do you feel that you have some of the qualities listed in

(1) combined with some of those listed in (2)? In common with most people, few of whom are *pure* introverts or extroverts, you are most likely an *ambivert.*

4. Is your mind so selfishly occupied with your own thoughts, desires, opinions, and needs as to make you indifferent to the interests of other folks? You are *egocentric.*

5. Do you often wish to do perfectly innocent, or perhaps not-so-innocent, things which your Puritan conscience, or your fear of ridicule, or your conservative upbringing, prevents you from doing? You are *inhibited.*

6. Are you so completely lacking in modesty and self-consciousness that you delight in making a spectacle of yourself? Do you make a play for the spotlight and are you eager to put on a one-man show at every gathering? You are an *exhibitionist.*

7. Do you always think of that witty remark *after* you get home? Do you feel that your opinions are not worth expressing? Are you so completely lacking in self-confidence that you rarely achieve the success or recognition that your talents and ability seem to deserve? You are *diffident.*

8. Are you generally sparkling, happy, bubbling over with zest and high spirits? You are *effervescent.*

9. Are you happiest when you are with a crowd? Do you prefer people to solitude and do you feel emotionally most content in the company of friends? You are *gregarious.*

10. Do you walk around with a chip on your shoulder? Are you always ready to do battle? Are you savage, fierce, ruthless, unyielding in your manner and in your arguments? You are *truculent.*

11. Are you grave, gloomy, heavy, foreboding? Do you rarely smile? You are *saturnine.*

12. Are you chivalrous, romantic and idealistic almost to a ridiculous extreme? Are you the opposite of practical? Do you place woman on so high a pedestal that she is unapproachable? Are you always chasing rainbows? You are *quixotic.*

II

To gain firmer control over these words, pronounce them aloud—several times!

1. *introvert* (IN´-trə-vurt´)
2. *extrovert* (EKS´-trō-vurt´)
3. *ambivert* (AM´-bee-vurt´)
4. *egocentric* (ee´-gō-SEN´-trik)
5. *inhibited* (in-HIB´-ə-təd)
6. *exhibitionist* (ek´-sə-BISH´-ə-nist)
7. *diffident* (DIF´-ə-dənt)
8. *effervescent* (ef´-ər-VESS´-ənt)
9. *gregarious* (grə-GAIR´-ee-əs)
10. *truculent* (TRUK´-yə-lənt)
11. *saturnine* (SAT´-ər-nine´)
12. *quixotic* (kwik-SOT´-ik)

III

Can you match each word to its definition? Initial letters will guide you. But don't look back, please.

1. Possessed with self-distrust; shy; timid   D _____
2. Bubbly and sparkling in personality   E _____
3. Looking at everything from a personal point of view
   E _____
4. Delight with putting on an act in front of others
   E _____
5. One whose chief interests are outside of himself and who makes friends easily   E _____
6. Preferring the company of others to solitude   G _____
7. One whose interest is directed inward, who is turned in upon himself, and who is much alone   I _____
8. Idealistic but unpractical   Q _____

9. Morose, gloomy, heavy, dull   S _____
10. Savage and pugnacious in character   T _____
11. One who finds his satisfactions both within and in the outside world   A _____
12. Held back by conscience, early training, fear, feelings of shyness, etc.   I _____

ANSWERS: (1) diffident; (2) effervescent; (3) egocentric; (4) exhibitionist; (5) extrovert; (6) gregarious; (7) introvert; (8) quixotic; (9) saturnine; (10) truculent; (11) ambivert; (12) inhibited

IV

Try once again, without initial letters.

1. Cruel, ferocious   _____
2. Shy and timid   _____
3. Bubbling over   _____
4. Considering self the center of everything   _____
5. Psychically restrained   _____
6. One who loves to be the center of attention   _____
7. One whose interests are directed outward   _____
8. Liking to be with other people   _____
9. One whose interest is directed inward   _____
10. Idealistic but impractical   _____
11. Gloomy and morose   _____
12. One who finds his satisfactions both inside and outside himself   _____

ANSWERS: (1) truculent; (2) diffident; (3) effervescent; (4) egocentric; (5) inhibited; (6) exhibitionist; (7) extrovert; (8) gregarious; (9) introvert; (10) quixotic; (11) saturnine; (12) ambivert

V

Nouns often end in such characteristic suffixes as *-tion* or *-sion, -ism, -ence, -ness,* and *-ity.* Can you figure out the noun form of each adjective?

1. *introverted* (as in: characterized by _____)
2. *extroverted* (as in: known for his _____)
3. *ambiverted* (as in: most people tend toward _____)
4. *egocentric* (as in: hated for his annoying _____)
5. *inhibited* (as in: a prey to oppressive _____)
6. *exhibitionistic* (as in: accused of _____)
7. *diffident* (as in: projects a poor image because of his _____)
8. *effervescent* (as in: delighted with his charm and _____)
9. *gregarious* (as in: a slave to his unending _____)
10. *truculent* (as in: cowed everyone with his _____)
11. *quixotic* (as in: such ridiculous _____)
12. *saturnine* (as in: oppressed by _____)

ANSWERS: (1) introversion; (2) extroversion; (3) ambiversion; (4) egocentricity *or* egocentrism; (5) inhibitedness *or* inhibition; (6) exhibitionism; (7) diffidence; (8) effervescence; (9) gregariousness; (10) truculence; (11) quixoticism; (12) saturninity (sat´-ər-NIN´-ə-tee)

With each chapter, your power over words is growing. And yet you are doing much more than merely learning lists of words. In addition to the new words you have learned, you have also opened up new avenues of thought for yourself. An improved vocabulary leads to enlarged horizons, new vistas, experience with ideas not previously experienced. It is no accident that successful and intelligent people have the largest vocabularies. Their competence with words is a token, a result, of their breadth of thinking and experience.

1̶	2̶	3̶	4̶	5̶	6̶	7̶
8̶	9̶	10̶	11̶	12̶	13̶	14̶
15̶	16̶	17̶	18̶	19̶	20	21
22	23	24	25	26	27	28
29	30					

Adjectives Give You Power

A vocabulary of power gives you the ability to condense a highly involved thought into a single word. Thus, if you wish to describe an action that is so ordinary and undistinguished and common that it immediately marks its perpetrator as a person completely lacking in imagination (notice how many words we have used to express this thought), you will use the word *plebeian*. On the other hand, an act that indicates excessive desire to be overattentive, with attendant evidence of insincerity and a suspicion of ulterior motives, might be characterized as *obsequious*. Again, an action that is sickeningly sentimental and indicative of emotional immaturity, and one that is often accompanied by tears, could be called *maudlin*.

I

There are many such words that compress a wealth of meaning and emotion into a few syllables. Note how expressive the following phrases are:

1. A *plebeian* (plə-BEE´-ən) outlook on life
2. *Obsequious* (ob-SEE´-kwee-əs) attentions of the headwaiter

3. A *maudlin* (MAWD´-lin) motion picture

4. A *perfunctory* (pər-FUNK´-tə-ree) examination by a busy doctor who has very little time for you

5. An *abortive* (ə-BAWR´-tiv) attempt to gain his ends

6. A *surreptitious* (sur´-rep-TISH´-əs) movement on the part of the thief

7. A *presumptuous* (prə-ZUMP´-choo-əs) question to put to the governor

8. The *sadistic* (sə-DISS´-tik) treatment of the prisoner by ruthless guards

9. A *flagrant* (FLAY´-grənt) misuse of company funds

10. An *inane* (in-AYN´) remark

II

From an analysis of the phrases you have just studied, write each word next to its definition:

1. Openly, glaringly wrong or scandalous _____

2. Senseless; silly; empty _____

3. Made foolish by liquor; tearfully affectionate or sentimental _____

4. Overcourteous and servile in manner _____

5. Done mechanically and without interest; superficial and careless _____

6. Unduly confident or bold; audacious; arrogant; taking too much for granted _____

7. Inclined to cruelty; getting pleasure out of hurting others _____

8. By secret or stealthy means _____

9. Common; coarse; vulgarly ordinary, mediocre, or commonplace _____

10. Coming to naught; failing _____

ANSWERS: (1) flagrant; (2) inane; (3) maudlin; (4) obsequious;
(5) perfunctory; (6) presumptuous; (7) sadistic; (8) surreptitious;
(9) plebeian; (10) abortive

III

Try the same method with another list of valuable and expressive
adjectives.

1. *Wanton* (WAHN´-tən) cruelty
2. *Crass* (KRASS´) behavior
3. *Macabre* (mə-KAH´-bər) mystery
4. *Dogmatic* (dog-MAT´-ik) assertion
5. *Vitriolic* (vit´-ree-OL´-ik) satire
6. *Intermittent* (in-tər-MIT´-ənt) ringing of the telephone
7. *Subversive* (səb-VUR´-siv) activities of people who
   wish to overthrow the government
8. *Desultory* (DESS´-əl-taw´-ree) flitting from one subject
   to another
9. A *sardonic* (sahr-DON´-ik) smile

IV

Again, from an analysis of the phrases in Section III, write each word
next to its definition.

1. Passing irregularly from one thing to another; changeable;
   without method or plan _____
2. Descriptive of an opinion stated in an overpositive and
   arrogant manner _____
3. Recklessly inconsiderate or heartless; unrestrained;
   extravagant _____
4. Stupid in a grossly inconsiderate way _____
5. Ceasing and starting again _____
6. Bitter, scornful, and sneering _____

7. Pertaining to, indicative of, or suggesting death; hence, gruesome, grim, ghastly, horrible _____

8. Extremely biting or sarcastic; figuratively caustic or bitter _____

9. Tending to overthrow from the very foundations, as of a moral or political force; aiming to destroy _____

ANSWERS: (1) desultory; (2) dogmatic; (3) wanton; (4) crass; (5) intermittent; (6) sardonic; (7) macabre; (8) vitriolic; (9) subversive

V

You will recall from the previous chapter that a noun often and characteristically ends in such suffixes as *-ity* (*saturninity*), *-ness* (*gregariousness*), *-ion* (*inhibition*), *-ism* (*asceticism*), *-ence* (*diffidence*), *-ance* (*circumstance*), *-ency* or *-ancy* (*potency, occupancy*), etc.

Adverbs end in *-ly*, as *diffidently, gregariously,* etc.

Can you change each adjective as required below?

1. *Obsequious* to a noun: "His _____ was annoying."

2. *Perfunctory* to an adverb: "He did his work _____."

3. *Surreptitious* to an adverb: "He crept through the house _____."

4. *Presumptuous* to a noun: "Your _____ will be punished."

5. *Sadistic* to a noun denoting the person: "He is a _____."

6. *Sadistic* to a noun denoting the philosophy: "He was a victim of his wife's _____."

7. *Flagrant* to a noun: "I cannot understand how you can break the law with such _____."

8. *Inane* to a plural noun: "His speech is full of _____."

9. *Wanton* to an adverb: "_____, she broke her husband's heart."

10. *Crass* to a noun: "His _____ makes it impossible for him to be accepted by refined people."

11. *Dogmatic* to a noun: "Why do you always speak with such _____?"

12. *Intermittent* to an adverb: "The rain came down _____."

13. *Desultory* to an adverb: "He works _____."

ANSWERS: (1) obsequiousness; (2) perfunctorily; (3) surreptitiously; (4) presumption *or* presumptuousness; (5) sadist; (6) sadism; (7) flagrancy; (8) inanities; (9) wantonly; (10) crassness *or* crassitude; (11) dogmatism *or* dogmaticness; (12) intermittently; (13) desultorily

VI

First, review all nineteen words carefully (including their noun and adverb forms), pronouncing them aloud once again to fix them in your mind. Then complete each of the following sentences with one of the words or forms that you think will fit best.

1. He made an _____ attempt to regain the governorship; his defeat left him a sad and bitter man who thereafter spoke _____ of his political past.

2. Can you think of anything quite so _____ cruel as war?

3. Pompous people delight in _____ attendance on their every wish.

4. Thievery will out, and anything you do _____ will some day be found out.

5. Please don't state so _____ that democracy is a fiasco. Time will show the stupidity of such a statement.

6. He disliked his job heartily, and therefore it was no surprise that he discharged his duties so _____.

7. With what malicious and _____ satisfaction the prosecutor made the witness reveal his past!

8. Read with a purpose; _____ reading is neither satisfactory nor sensible.

9. During a political campaign, candidates often descend to making _____ attacks on their opponents.

10. It was an overcast day, with only _____ sunshine.

11. This error is so glaring and _____ that I'm amazed you didn't catch it.

12. Isn't it rather _____ for a person of your reputation to ask to be my friend?

13. He has a _____ tongue; his biting sarcasm has alienated everyone who knows him.

14. Peaceful people are aghast at the _____ destruction of life and property that occurs during wars and riots.

15. He made a futile, _____ attempt at rescue.

16. Such _____ materialism will never lead to real happiness.

ANSWERS: (1) abortive, sardonically; (2) wantonly; (3) obsequious; (4) surreptitiously; (5) dogmatically; (6) perfunctorily; (7) sadistic; (8) desultory; (9) flagrant, inane, wanton, crass, *or* vitriolic; (10) intermittent; (11) flagrant; (12) presumptuous; (13) vitriolic; (14) wanton; (15) abortive; (16) crass

The answers given above are not necessarily the only possible ones. In some of the sentences several of the words will fit. As a person whose vocabulary is becoming daily larger and larger, you realize that there are a multitude of ways of saying the same thing. But the particular word you choose will determine the flavor of your thought. This is the priceless value of a large vocabulary. Out of your wide range of words you can pick and choose the exact term that will best express each subtle nuance in your mind.

VII

Now a quick and final run-through to reinforce your learning. Is each pair of words nearly the *same* or more nearly *opposed* in meaning?

1. *plebeian* unusual Same___ Opposed___
2. *obsequious* brusque Same___ Opposed___
3. *maudlin* sentimental Same___ Opposed___
4. *perfunctory* superficial Same___ Opposed___
5. *abortive* successful Same___ Opposed___
6. *surreptitious* aboveboard Same___ Opposed___
7. *presumptuous* humble Same___ Opposed___
8. *sadistic* cruel Same___ Opposed___
9. *flagrant* hidden Same___ Opposed___
10. *inane* meaningful Same___ Opposed___
11. *wanton* restrained Same___ Opposed___
12. *crass* refined Same___ Opposed___
13. *macabre* eerie Same___ Opposed___
14. *dogmatic* opinionated Same___ Opposed___
15. *vitriolic* sarcastic Same___ Opposed___
16. *intermittent* continuous Same___ Opposed___
17. *subversive* protective Same___ Opposed___
18. *desultory* aimless Same___ Opposed___
19. *sardonic* bitter Same___ Opposed___

ANSWERS: (1) opposed; (2) opposed; (3) same; (4) same; (5) opposed; (6) opposed; (7) opposed; (8) same; (9) opposed; (10) opposed; (11) opposed; (12) opposed; (13) same; (14) same; (15) same; (16) opposed; (17) opposed; (18) same; (19) same

X	X	X	X	X	X	X
X	X	10	11	12	13	14
15	16	17	18	19	20	21
22	23	24	25	26	27	28
29	30					

Learning Words the Modern Way

This book is not a memory course.

Merely memorizing lists of words by rote happens to be the slowest and most difficult way to remember them. If you follow such a routine you will find that you have forgotten most of the list by the next day.

What, then, is the correct procedure?

Just this.

Look at the word first, if you can, in its context: in the paragraph where it appears. The very sense of the paragraph will give you an inkling of the significance of the word—even if you have never seen it before. You naturally become eager to know the definition of the word in order to understand the sentence pattern in which you have seen it. Your approach, then, is *indirect and psychological,* because you wish the information, not as an end in itself, but as a means to an end. You realize that if you learn the meaning of the word you will comprehend the meaning of the sentence. You are using what is called the modern *inductive* method, in that you first discover the word at work, you are challenged by it, you guess at its meaning, and you then confirm or correct your guess by referring to the dictionary.

When you use this method, the words are no longer so much dead wood, to be piled up in your mind, but are living entities, charged with action and emotion. They then become hard to forget.

Let's be specific and illustrate our point.

We will discuss thirteen adverbs and two adverbial phrases and try to prove how much easier it is to learn by the *indirect, inductive, and psychological* route.

I

Give your careful attention to the following sentences in Groups A, B, C, D, and E. In each sentence you will find an adverb in italics. If the word is new to you, try to guess at its meaning.

GROUP A

1. He complained *acrimoniously*.
2. We argued *acrimoniously*.
3. They mocked each other *acrimoniously*.
   (You can feel the unpleasant overtone of this word, can't you?)

GROUP B

1. He completed the operation *adroitly*.
2. He drove *adroitly* through the maze of traffic.
3. *Adroitly* she knitted the complicated stitch.
   (This word obviously applies to some manual action.)

GROUP C

1. He moved slowly and *circumspectly* through the range of fire.
2. Fearing a trick, he answered all questions *circumspectly*.
3. By walking *circumspectly*, he avoided an ambush.
   (There's a feeling of watchfulness about this word.)

GROUP D

1. These two building leases run *concomitantly*.
2. Living and learning go on *concomitantly*.
3. Rain, snow, and sleet, all came down *concomitantly*.
   (You probably know why two or more things *must* be
   involved in these actions, even if you happen never to have
   seen the word before.)

GROUP E

1. He examined the plans *cursorily*.
2. He ran through the pages *cursorily*, then threw the
   novel down in disgust.
3. He did his homework so *cursorily* that he flunked his
   examination.
   (This word should carry an impression of superficial
   haste.)

II

Now pronounce the words aloud.

1. *acrimoniously* (ak´-rə-MŌ´-nee-əs-lee)
2. *adroitly* (ə-DROYT´-lee)
3. *circumspectly* (sur´-kəm-SPEKT´-lee)
4. *concomitantly* (kon-KOM´-ə-tənt-lee)
5. *cursorily* (KUR´-sə-rə-lee)

III

Let us try five more words, using the same intriguing and productive
method. Again, try to figure out the probable meanings of the italicized
words.

1. Teachers are apt to talk *didactically*.
2. Extremely modest persons usually speak of their own
   accomplishments *disparagingly*.

3. People with extremely facile and ready tongues can talk *glibly.*
4. The person who is looking for sympathy talks *plaintively.*
5. Pessimists usually speak *ominously* of the future.

IV

Pronounce them:

1. *didactically* (dy´-DAK´-tik-lee)
2. *disparagingly* (dis-PAIR´-ə-jing-ly)
3. *glibly* (GLIB´-lee)
4. *plaintively* (PLAIN´-tiv-lee)
5. *ominously* (OM´-ə-nəs-lee)

V

And still another five, in the same way.

1. Man cannot break the laws of nature with *impunity.*
2. He placed his hand on the hot radiator *inadvertently.*
3. He was a disagreeable old man who answered every question *irascibly.*
4. Inasmuch as the plans were executed *sub rosa*, the stockholders realized too late how completely they had been defrauded.
5. He never gave up quietly. He always complained *vociferously* if he thought he had been treated unfairly.

VI

Pronounce them:

1. *impunity* (im-PYOO-nə-tee)
2. *inadvertently* (in-ad-VUR´-tənt-lee)
3. *irascibly* (i-RASS´-ə-blee)
4. *sub rosa* (sub-RŌ´-zə)
5. *vociferously* (vō-SIF´-ə-rəs-lee)

VII

Okay. You have looked at, thought about, and tried to understand fifteen useful adverbial expressions. Now take the next step in the learning process: *Write* the word (or phrase) in the blank line next to its definition. Initial letters are offered as guides.

1. Expertly; dexterously; with skillful use of the hands or mind A _____

2. Accompanying; occurring together C _____

3. In the fashion of a teacher; as if teaching a lesson D _____

4. In a manner of smooth ease and fluency; without hesitation G _____

5. In a heedless manner; without care; inattentively I _____

6. Forebodingly; in a way portending evil O _____

7. In strict confidence; privately S _____

8. In a loud-voiced manner; vehemently; noisily V _____

9. Expressing sadness or melancholy P _____

10. Angrily; irritably; in hot-tempered fashion I _____

11. With freedom from punishment or injurious consequences with I _____

12. Speaking slightingly of, in a way to undervalue and discredit D _____

13. Hastily and superficially, without due care and attention C _____

14. Cautiously with watchfulness in all directions C _____

15. With sharpness and bitterness of speech or temper A _____

ANSWERS: (1) adroitly; (2) concomitantly; (3) didactically; (4) glibly; (5) inadvertently; (6) ominously; (7) sub rosa; (8) vociferously; (9) plaintively; (10) irascibly; (11) with impunity; (12) disparagingly; (13) cursorily; (14) circumspectly; (15) acrimoniously

VIII

Next, you reinforce your learning even more. Here are forty-six synonyms or synonymous phrases that fit the thirteen adverbs and two adverbial phrases you have been working on. Each adverb or adverbial phrase will be required two or more times. Can you go through this exercise happily, smoothly, and with an increasing sense of confidence and power? You are on your own, with no initial letters to help you.

1. hastily _____

2. warily _____

3. in a teacher-like manner _____

4. irritably _____

5. in a way foreboding evil _____

6. sadly _____

7. in a hidden manner _____

8. loudly _____

9. inauspiciously _____

10. angrily _____

11. dexterously _____

12. cautiously _____

13. slightingly _____

14. fluently _____

15. caustically _____

16. heedlessly _____

17. at the same time _____

18. with anger and annoyance _____

19. prudently _____

20. with exemption from punishment _____

21. smoothly _____

22. stingingly _____

23. thoughtlessly _____

24. deprecatingly _____

25. conjointly _____

26. without danger of punishment _____

27. bitterly _____

28. unhesitatingly _____

29. depreciatively _____

30. skillfully _____

31. irately _____

32. in a way expressing coming danger or misfortune _____

33. sorrowfully _____

34. without incurring penalty, harm, or loss _____

35. rapidly and hastily _____

36. like an instructor _____

37. mournfully _____

38. secretly _____

39. clamorously _____

40. in loud tones _____

41. noisily _____

42. instructively _____

43. confidentially _____

44. in a melancholy way _____

45. belittlingly _____

46. superficially _____

ANSWERS: (1) cursorily; (2) circumspectly; (3) didactically;
(4) irascibly; (5) ominously; (6) plaintively; (7) sub rosa;
(8) vociferously; (9) ominously; (10) irascibly; (11) adroitly;
(12) circumspectly; (13) disparagingly; (14) glibly;
(15) acrimoniously; (16) inadvertently; (17) concomitantly;
(18) irascibly; (19) circumspectly; (20) with impunity; (21) glibly;
(22) acrimoniously; (23) inadvertently; (24) disparagingly;
(25) concomitantly; (26) with impunity; (27) acrimoniously;
(28) glibly; (29) disparagingly; (30) adroitly; (31) irascibly;
(32) ominously; (33) plaintively; (34) with impunity; (35) cursorily;

(36) didactically; (37) plaintively; (38) sub rosa; (39) vociferously; (40) vociferously; (41) vociferously; (42) didactically; (43) sub rosa; (44) plaintively; (45) disparagingly; (46) cursorily

IX

Find an adverb or adverbial phrase that will best fit each of the seven situations described below.

1. You are a burglar. You have just entered a wealthy home through an unlocked window. All is dark, and alas, you have forgotten to bring your flashlight with you. To add to your troubles, you can't find the electric switch. How will you move around in this room until you can get your bearings? _____

2. You are an irritable, touchy old man, and as you walk along the street on this cold, raw morning you feel nothing but enmity toward the whole world. A beggar stops you for a coin. How do you refuse? _____

3. A friend has been importuning you for weeks to look over a novel he is writing and give him your criticism. Knowing your friend, you are certain that the novel is bad even before you read it; besides, you are very busy. Rather than give your friend a blunt refusal, however, you take the manuscript home one evening. How do you examine it? _____

4. Your small son wishes to know why it snows. You are well versed in the natural sciences and have made it a habit to answer all your son's questions as clearly and accurately as possible. How do you answer him? _____

5. You have influence with the chief of police, and furthermore, your wife is the mayor's daughter. Consequently, you never trouble to obey traffic laws. In fact, you can break them _____.

6. A woman has broken your heart purposely, and with malice aforethought. She has left you a disillusioned man. It takes you years even to begin to get over it. And then one day you meet her again. She is elated, debonair; she has obviously forgotten what she has done to you. This angers you and you intend to sting her when you remind her. In what fashion do you speak to her? _____

7. You are a very modest person. Rather than praise anything you have done, you prefer to take as little credit as possible for your accomplishments. How do you usually speak of yourself? _____

ANSWERS: (1) circumspectly; (2) irascibly; (3) cursorily; (4) didactically; (5) with impunity; (6) acrimoniously; (7) disparagingly

X

An important step in improving your vocabulary is to practice changing parts of speech. Drop the *-ly* of the thirteen adverbs and you have adjectives; choose the proper suffix (*-ness, -ion, -ence, -ance, -ism, -ity*) and you can form a noun from the adjective.

By the way, two noun endings we have not yet discussed will be required in this exercise, *-ony* (as in *ceremony*, from the adjective *ceremonious*) and *-ment* (as in *development*, from the adjective *developing*).

Ready to turn adverbs into nouns?

1. *acrimoniously* _____
2. *adroitly* _____
3. *circumspectly* _____
4. *concomitantly* _____
5. *cursorily* _____
6. *didactically* _____
7. *disparagingly* _____

8. *glibly* _____

9. *plaintively* _____

10. *ominously* _____

11. *inadvertently* _____

12. *irascibly* _____

13. *vociferously* _____

ANSWERS: (1) acrimony; (2) adroitness; (3) circumspection;
(4) concomitance; (5) cursoriness; (6) didacticism; (7) disparagement;
(8) glibness; (9) plaintiveness; (10) ominousness; (11) inadvertence;
(12) irascibility; (13) vociferousness

Most adjectives can be made into nouns by adding -*ness,* although this is not always the most sophisticated suffix. Therefore, alternate forms for 1, 3, 4, 6, 7, 11, and 12 are *acrimoniousness, circumspectness, concomitantness* (not the happiest of choices), *didacticness, disparagingness* (again, awkward), *inadvertentness* (awkward), and *irascibleness.*

Occasionally you may feel that these exercises are time-consuming. But we urge you never to let the lack of time stand as an obstacle to this work. Thomas Carlyle, the great philosopher, claimed that there is time in everyone's life for a career within a career. Even so-called geniuses are geniuses largely because they are willing to use the time that others throw away. It was Michelangelo who said: "If people only knew how hard I work to gain my mastery it wouldn't seem so wonderful at all." And Alexandre Dumas, the transcendent French novelist, confessed: "Infatuated, half through conceit, half through love of my art, I achieve the impossible working as none else ever works. . . ."

Careers are not had by wishing and hoping. They are *earned* through work and enthusiasm.

~~1~~	~~2~~	~~3~~	~~4~~	~~5~~	~~6~~	~~7~~
~~8~~	~~9~~	~~10~~	~~11~~	~~12~~	~~13~~	~~14~~
~~15~~	~~16~~	~~17~~	~~18~~	~~19~~	~~20~~	~~21~~
22	23	24	25	26	27	28
29	30					

Words from Latin

A large part of our English vocabulary, as we know, derives from Latin. This language is no longer used except in the somewhat modified form of "Church Latin." Old Latin was no longer a spoken tongue when modern English began; yet English is such a vital and avid tongue that it has steadily fed upon Latin, and even today this Roman speech is constantly taken over into English by scholars, philologists, and scientists.

Any time you run an inquisitive plow through our language you turn up Latin roots everywhere.

I

There is the simple word *animal*. Why particularly do we use the word *animal* instead of some other combination of syllables?

Animal is from the Latin *anima*, "mind," "breath," "soul," or "spirit," and of course, animals, as opposed to minerals or *inanimate* objects, do breathe and do possess that mysterious something that gives them a life not found in "inanimate" things. The root *anima* is found in a host of common English words:

*animal*cule—a tiny live thing
*anima*te—to breathe life into
equ*anim*ity—equal or placid spirit or mind
magn*anim*ous—of large, or noble, spirit
un*anim*ous—of one mind
in*anim*ate—without a soul; hence, not alive
*anim*osity—vehement enmity: literally, with one's mind against
pusill*anim*ous—fainthearted; cowardly: literally, of small mind
*anim*advert—to turn the mind to; to notice; to criticize

II

In many cases, English words are formed by combining parts of two or more Latin words. Thus "equanimity" is a fusion of *aequus,* "equal," and *anima.* You will recognize the root *aequus* (spelled *equ-* or *-iqu* in English) in such words as *equation, equality, equity,* and *iniquity. Magnanimous* combines *magnus,* "large," with *anima.* Engage in a little etymological exploration, if you will, and see what other words you can turn up with the stem of *magnus,* "large."

1. _____ A person large in importance, as in an industry
2. _____ To make large
3. _____ Splendor; grandeur
4. _____ Speaking big or in pompous or flowery style
5. _____ Bigness or greatness
6. _____ A large bottle (two quarts) for champagne or other wine
7. _____ A great work; a literary or artistic work of importance

ANSWERS: (1) magnate; (2) magnify; (3) magnificence; (4) magniloquent; (5) magnitude; (6) magnum; (7) magnum opus

III

Let us pronounce the words we have discovered so far. For best results, say them aloud several times.

1. *animalcule* (AN´-ə-məl-kyool´)
2. *animate,* verb: (AN´-ə-mayt´)
   adjective: (AN´-ə-mət)
3. *equanimity* (ee´-kwə-NIM´-ə-tee)
4. *magnanimous* (mag-NAN´-ə-məs)
5. *unanimous* (yōō-NAN´-ə-məs)
6. *inanimate* (in-AN´-ə-mət)
7. *animosity* (an´-ə-MOS´-ə-tee)
8. *pusillanimous* (pyōō´-sə-LAN´-ə-məs)
9. *animadvert* (AN´-ə-məd-vert´)
10. *magnate* (MAG´-nayt)
11. *magnify* (MAG´-nə-fy)
12. *magnificence* (mag-NIF´-ə-sənce)
13. *magniloquent* (mag-NIL´-ə-kwənt)
14. *magnitude* (MAG´-nə-tōōd´)
15. *magnum* (MAG´-nəm)
16. *magnum opus* (MAG´-nəm-O´-pəs)

IV

Now, to give you practice in spelling these words and to reinforce your learning, we ask you to write the word that fits each definition.

1. Large-minded; not petty   M _____
2. Small-minded; cowardly   P _____
3. Strong hostility   A _____
4. To invest with life   A _____
5. Make larger   M _____
6. Without life   I _____
7. Turn one's mind to   A _____

8. Agreed to by everyone   U _____
9. Using flowery language   M _____
10. Placid, unruffled temperament   E _____
11. Great literary or artistic work   M _____
      O _____
12. Two-quart bottle   M _____
13. Largeness; large size   M _____
14. Greatness; grandeur   M _____
15. Important person in industry   M _____
16. Very small creature   A _____

ANSWERS: (1) magnanimous; (2) pusillanimous; (3) animosity;
(4) animate; (5) magnify; (6) inanimate; (7) animadvert; (8) unanimous;
(9) magniloquent; (10) equanimity; (11) magnum opus; (12) magnum;
(13) magnitude; (14) magnificence; (15) magnate; (16) animalcule

V

Unanimous combines *unus*, "one," with *anima*, "mind." Can you think of
some other English words which contain *unus*?

1. _____   Make into one
2. _____   A fabulous animal with a single, straight horn
3. _____   Of one form or kind
4. _____   The state of being united
5. _____   Descriptive of the only one of its kind
6. _____   Harmony; also, a joining together in sound
7. _____   A single one

ANSWERS: (1) unify *or* unite; (2) unicorn; (3) uniform; (4) union, unity,
or unification; (5) unique; (6) unison; (7) unit

VI

Pronounce the new words:

1. *unify* (YOO′-nə-fy′)
2. *unite* (yoo-NITE′)

3. *unicorn* (Y$\overline{OO}$′-nə-kawrn)

4. *uniform* (Y$\overline{OO}$′-nə-fawrm)

5. *union* (Y$\overline{OO}$N′-yən)

6. *unity* (Y$\overline{OO}$′-nə-tee)

7.. *unification* (y$\overline{oo}$-nə-fə-KAY′-shən)

8. *unique* (y$\overline{oo}$-NEEK′)

9. *unison* (Y$\overline{OO}$′-nə-sən)

10. *unit* (Y$\overline{OO}$′-nit)

VII

Continuing our etymological exploration, let us next consider the word *benevolence*. Its meaning—"a feeling of goodwill toward others" or "a charitable action for the benefit of others"—can be understood better when we analyze the two Latin roots that have been welded together to form the word: *bene*, "well," and *volens*, "wishing." *Benevolence* means, literally, "wishing others well." *Bene* is found in other words. Here are a few:

*bene*fit

*bene*ficiary

*bene*diction

*bene*factor

The root *volens*, "wishing," also appears frequently:

*vol*ition

*vol*untary

*vol*unteer

If we now dissect two of the words containing *bene*, we will discover that new Latin roots can easily be added to our repertoire; *benediction*, "a blessing," is, literally, a "saying well." The root *dic* is from Latin *dicere*, "to say" or "to tell." You can see it in the following words:

*dic*tate

*dic*taphone

diction

male*diction*

in*dict*

pre*dict*

Again, *benefactor*, literally "well-doer," contains the Latin *facere*, "to do" or "to make." Watch how this root is employed in the following words.

factor

manu*facture*

fact

factotum

factual

VIII

Thus, the study of a few of these simple words brings to light eight new roots. Here are the Latin roots with their meanings. Can you recall an English word using each root?

	ROOT	MEANING	EXAMPLE
1.	*anima*	soul, spirit, mind	_____
2.	*aequus*	even, equal	_____
3.	*magnus*	large, big, great	_____
4.	*unus*	one, single	_____
5.	*bene*	well	_____
6.	*volens*	wishing	_____
7.	*facere*	to do, to make	_____
8.	*dicere*	to say, to tell	_____

IX

Can you recall the other Greek and Latin roots that you have learned in previous chapters? In the chart below you will find a list of them, each with an example. Can you fill in the English meaning of each root?

	ROOT	EXAMPLE	MEANING
1.	*monos*	*monocle*	_____
2.	*bis*	*bicycle*	_____
3.	*polys*	*polygamy*	_____
4.	*misein*	*misogyny*	_____
5.	*gamos*	*bigamy*	_____
6.	*theos*	*monotheism*	_____
7.	*anthropos*	*anthropology*	_____
8.	*philein*	*philatelist*	_____
9.	*logos*	*philology*	_____
10.	*cuspis*	*bicuspid*	_____
11.	*glotta*	*polyglot*	_____

ANSWERS: (1) one; (2) twice, two; (3) many; (4) to hate; (5) marriage; (6) God; (7) man; (8) to love; (9) study of, word; (10) point; (11) tongue

You will find it excellent practice to keep a weather eye out for these roots and for their various and varied combinations in your daily reading. There are so many of them that it becomes a fascinating sport to try to trace them. There is the Latin word *signum*, or "sign," which gives us in*sign*ia, the signs you wear; *sign*al, a sign; *sign*ify, make a sign; and such others as de*sign*, *sign*ature, in*sign*ificant. We also have the Latin *portare*, "to carry," which leads to *port*er, one who carries; *port*able, able to be carried; re*port*er, one who carries news back; de*port*, carry away; im*port*, carry in; and ex*port*, carry out.

A knowledge of Latin and Greek roots is a splendid vocabulary stretcher.

X̶	X̶	X̶	X̶	X̶	X̶	X̶
X̶	X̶	1̶0̶	1̶1̶	1̶2̶	1̶3̶	1̶4̶
1̶5̶	1̶6̶	1̶7̶	1̶8̶	1̶9̶	2̶0̶	2̶1̶
2̶2̶	23	24	25	26	27	28
29	30					

Test Your Progress

There is one thing that we cannot overemphasize in this daily word study, and that is the high importance of continually reviewing the work that you have done. New words that come into your vocabulary are as elusive as little shining eels, and unless you rehearse them constantly you will find that they will wriggle out from between your mental fingers and slip back into the sea of language.

If you want to make swift progress, take each page of this book seriously, review your work as a matter of course, and so secure the ground as you proceed.

Here is another hint. Be sure to finish this book. Forty-nine out of fifty persons don't thoroughly finish what they begin. This is what will make success so easy for you. Use your willpower. Willpower is often just another name for courage. Perseverance is energy made habitual. And perseverance, continuously applied, may become genius. So don't just finish this book—or this chapter—and lay it aside. Put it to work. Too many people are forever learning and never doing.

Right now we are going to challenge you with a review of Chapters

X to XXI. The tests that follow will not be easy, for they are intended to show up any weak spots in your methods of study.

I

Match the descriptions in Column B to the words in Column A.

A.		B.	
1.	*atheist*	a.	Loud-mouthed woman
2.	*virtuoso*	b.	Connoisseur of good food
3.	*virago*	c.	Disbeliever in God
4.	*gourmet*	d.	Beginner
5.	*tyro*	e.	One who leads an austere life
6.	*philatelist*	f.	Stamp collector
7.	*ascetic*	g.	Traitor
8.	*pedant*	h.	Boot-licker
9.	*judas*	i.	Skilled practitioner of the arts
10.	*sycophant*	j.	One who is ostentatious about his learning

II

Write the word with the indicated initial letter that satisfies each definition.

1. Insane desire to set fires   P _____
2. Uncontrollable propensity to steal   K _____
3. Forgetfulness of the past   A _____
4. Sleepwalking   S _____
5. Alternating fits of despondency and hilarity   M _____
6. Split personality   S _____
7. Fear of closed spaces   C _____
8. Continuous drunkenness   D _____
9. Persecution complex   P _____
10. Fear of large spaces   A _____

III

Choose the word in group A that satisfies each of the definitions in Group B.

A   *lethargy   weltschmerz   superciliousness*
    nostalgia   antipathy   vindictiveness
    benevolence   compunction   misogyny
    satiety   enervation   misanthropy
    frustration   ennui   vicariousness

B   1. Homesickness _____
    2. Goodwill to all _____
    3. Repletion _____
    4. Thwarting _____
    5. Dislike _____
    6. World-sorrow _____
    7. Hatred of women _____
    8. Scruple _____
    9. Revengefulness _____
    10. Haughtiness _____
    11. Sluggishness _____
    12. Exhaustion _____
    13. Boredom _____
    14. Hatred of mankind _____
    15. Indirect experience _____

IV

Write in the science that deals with each of the following subjects. The initial letter is given.

1. Mankind   A _____ *logy*
2. Rocks   G _____ *logy*
3. Ancient relics   A _____ *logy*
4. Unborn babies   E _____ *logy*

5. Insects   E _____ logy
6. Distribution of races   E _____ logy
7. Derivation of words   E _____ logy
8. Birds   O _____ logy
9. Languages   P _____ logy
10. The human mind   P _____ logy

V

Here are two columns of ten words each. Where the words opposite each other are synonyms, write the letter "S" between the pair. Where they have opposite meanings, write "O." Where the words have no relationship to each other, write "N."

1. *loquacious* ____ talkative
2. *gullible* ____ shrewd
3. *suave* ____ happy
4. *pompous* ____ conceited
5. *taciturn* ____ silent
6. *phlegmatic* ____ excitable
7. *erudite* ____ ignorant
8. *complacent* ____ constant
9. *punctilious* ____ careless
10. *indefatigable* ____ tireless

VI

In column A are ten definitions; in column B are ten blanks, each with an initial and final letter. The definitions in column A and the words to be supplied in column B do not necessarily face each other. It is up to you to unscramble the columns and fill in the remaining letters of each word. For instance, start with number 1, "minor indiscretion." Now run down column B and see if (with the initial and last letters to guide you) you can recall the word that the phrase "minor indiscretion" describes. When you succeed in remembering it, fill it in.

A.	B.
1. minor indiscretion	1. P _____ y
2. poverty	2. M _____ r
3. boastfulness	3. J _____ m
4. cure-all	4. B _____ o
5. failure	5. P _____ a
6. characteristic peculiarity	6. P _____ o
7. irregularity	7. F _____ o
8. warmongering	8. A _____ y
9. pretend illness	9. C _____ y
10. trickery	10. I _____ y

VII

Match the two columns.

A.	B.
1. one whose mind is turned inward	a. *diffident*
2. self-centered	b. *extrovert*
3. restrained	c. *inhibited*
4. modest	d. *saturnine*
5. bubbling over with high spirits	e. *egocentric*
6. company-loving	f. *quixotic*
7. fierce; overbearing	g. *introvert*
8. gloomy	h. *effervescent*
9. extravagantly chivalrous	i. *truculent*
10. one whose mind is turned outward	j. *gregarious*

VIII

In each of the five lines below there is one word that correctly expresses the meaning given in the word or words in italics just ahead. Check a, b, or c.

1. *common, ordinary:* a. plebeian, b. obsequious, c. maudlin
2. *miserably failing:* a. perfunctory, b. abortive, c. surreptitious

3. *cruel:* a. presumptuous, b. sadistic, c. flagrant
4. *vulgar:* a. inane, b. wanton, c. crass
5. *biting:* a. macabre, b. dogmatic, c. vitriolic

IX

Proceed as in Test VIII.

1. *at the same time:* a. acrimoniously, b. adroitly, c. concomitantly
2. *carefully:* a. circumspectly, b. cursorily, c. didactically
3. *smoothly:* a. disparagingly, b. glibly, c. plaintively
4. *threateningly:* a. ominously, b. with impunity, c. inadvertently
5. *secretly:* a. irascibly, b. sub rosa, c. vociferously

X

Write the English meaning of each italicized Greek or Latin root.

1. *magn*animous _____
2. *un*ique _____
3. un*anim*ous _____
4. *bene*fit _____
5. bene*vol*ence _____
6. *dict*aphone _____
7. manu*fact*ure _____
8. mono*gamy* _____
9. *theo*logy _____
10. *bi*cycle _____

ANSWERS:

I: (1) c; (2) i; (3) a; (4) b; (5) d; (6) f; (7) e; (8) j; (9) g; (10) h

II: (1) pyromania; (2) kleptomania; (3) amnesia; (4) somnambulism; (5) manic-depression; (6) schizophrenia; (7) claustrophobia; (8) dipsomania; (9) paranoia; (10) agoraphobia

III: (1) nostalgia; (2) benevolence; (3) satiety; (4) frustration;
(5) antipathy; (6) weltschmerz; (7) misogyny; (8) compunction;
(9) vindictiveness; (10) superciliousness; (11) lethargy; (12) enervation;
(13) ennui; (14) misanthropy; (15) vicariousness

IV: (1) anthropology; (2) geology; (3) archaeology; (4) embryology;
(5) entomology; (6) ethnology; (7) etymology; (8) ornithology;
(9) philology; (10) psychology

V: (1) S; (2) O; (3) N; (4) S; (5) S; (6) O; (7) O; (8) N; (9) O; (10) S

VI: (1) penury; (2) malinger; (3) jingoism; (4) braggadocio;
(5) panacea; (6) peccadillo; (7) fiasco; (8) anomaly; (9) chicanery;
(10) idiosyncrasy

VII: (1) g; (2) e; (3) c; (4) a; (5) h; (6) j; (7) i; (8) d; (9) f; (10) b

VIII: (1) a; (2) b; (3) b; (4) c; (5) c

IX: (1) c; (2) a; (3) b; (4) a; (5) b

X: (1) large; (2) one; (3) mind or spirit; (4) well; (5) wish; (6) say;
(7) make; (8) marriage; (9) God; (10) two, twice

Scoring: one point for each correct answer
Maximum score: 95

Your Score: _____

80–95 Excellent
70–79 Good
51–69 Passing
0–50 Poor

If your score isn't as creditable as you would like, don't feel the least bit discouraged. And whatever your age, don't use the excuse that "you can't teach an old dog new tricks."

This ancient belief was entirely disproved by an exhaustive series of tests conducted under the direction of Dr. Irving Lorge, who was a brilliant psychologist at Columbia University. He established the fact that the human mind retains its full powers up to the most advanced age. The *speed* of thinking is usually a little less, but *without exception,* the power element shows no decline whatsoever with people even up to ninety years of age.

So Dr. Lorge deprived us of the easy and comfortable alibi of age!

X̶1	X̶2	X̶3	X̶4	X̶5	X̶6	X̶7
X̶8	X̶9	X̶10	X̶11	X̶12	X̶13	X̶14
X̶15	X̶16	X̶17	X̶18	X̶19	X̶20	X̶21
X̶22	X̶23	24	25	26	27	28
29	30					

Can You Meet This Challenge?

Continuing the inductive, psychological, and indirect method of building vocabulary that we discussed in Chapter XX, we shall now throw you pell-mell into a quiz to test your understanding of a group of words before going on to consider them. In each of the fifteen sentences that follow you will find one or two words in italics. If the words are strange to you, read the sentence carefully. Then, in each case, put a check after the particular phrase—*a, b,* or *c*—that you think comes nearest the meaning.

I

1. If spelling is your *bête noire,*
    a. You love spelling.
    b. You are a good speller.
    c. You hate spelling.
2. If your friend looked *cadaverous,* you would say to him:
    a. When do you head out?
    b. Better stop eating so many sweets.
    c. What cemetery do you live in?

3. If the president wants *carte blanche* in allocating defense funds,

   a. He wishes no strings to be attached to the money.

   b. He does not want special funds earmarked.

   c. He wants instructions from Congress on how to spend.

4. *Esoteric* knowledge is

   a. Knowledge possessed by a few.

   b. Useless knowledge.

   c. Knowledge that was buried with the fall of ancient civilization.

5. The man who says that psychology is his *forte* means

   a. He hates the subject.

   b. He's particularly good in the subject.

   c. He loves the subject.

6. When you come to an *impasse,*

   a. Stop, look, and listen!

   b. You find yourself completely blocked in a certain situation.

   c. Wait for a guide to show you the way out.

7. *Incongruous* means

   a. Out of place or character.

   b. Not honest.

   c. Not useful.

8. *Docile* people are

   a. Stupid.

   b. Lovable.

   c. Easily managed.

9. *Stratification* is placing something into

   a. Different groups.

   b. Numerical order.

   c. Drawers.

10. *Moribund* institutions

   a. Are passing out of existence.

  b. Are in charge of dishonest people.

  c. Are undemocratic.

11. A *nebulous* idea is one that is

  a. Heaven-sent.

  b. Vague.

  c. As pure as clouds.

12. People who indulge in *recriminations* are probably

  a. Playing a game.

  b. Quarreling.

  c. Writing letters.

13. The *repercussions* of an event must happen

  a. Before.

  b. After.

  c. At the same time.

14. *Scurrilous* language would more than likely be heard in

  a. The halls of Congress.

  b. A quarrel between two stevedores.

  c. A sermon.

15. *Soporific* speakers tend to

  a. Stimulate you to action.

  b. Appeal to your nobler instincts.

  c. Put you to sleep.

ANSWERS: (1) c; (2) c; (3) a; (4) a; (5) b; (6) b; (7) a; (8) c; (9) a; (10) a;
(11) b; (12) b; (13) b; (14) b; (15) c

II

Now pronounce the words—several times. Hear them in your own voice and you begin to feel more and more at home with them!

  1. *bête noire* (bet-NWAHR´)

  2. *cadaverous* (kə-DAV´-ə-rəs)

  3. *carte blanche* (kart-BLAHNSH´)

  4. *esoteric* (es´-ə-TAIR´-ik)

5. *forte* (for-TAY´)

6. *impasse* (IM´-pass)

7. *incongruous* (in-KONG´-grōō-əs)

    noun, *incongruity:* (in´-kəng-GRŌŌ´-ə-tee)

8. *docile* (DOSS´-əl)

    noun, *docility:* (doss-SIL´-ə-tee)

9. *stratification* (stra-tə-fə-KAY´-shən)

10. *moribund* (MAWR´-ə-bund´ *or* MAHR´-ə-bund´)

11. *nebulous* (NEB´-yə-ləs)

12. *recrimination* (rə-krim´-ə-NAY´-shən)

13. *repercussion* (rep´-ər-KUSH´-ən)

14. *scurrilous* (SKUR´-ə-ləs)

15. *soporific* (sop´-ə-RIF´-ik)

III

You've mulled the words and their meanings over in your mind. You've said them aloud. Now write them, one to each definition. (Some of the words may be required more than once.)

1. A particular object of hate or dread   B _____

2. Pale; ghastly   C _____

3. Unconditional permission or authority   C _____

4. Confined to a select circle   E _____

5. One's strong point   F _____

6. Corpselike   C _____

7. A blind alley; an insurmountable obstacle   I _____

8. For the initiated few   E _____

9. Inadaptable; out of place   I _____

10. Tractable   D _____

11. Dead end   I _____

12. An object of dread   B _____

13. Arrangement into different groups   S _____

14. In a dying state   M _____

15. Hazy; indistinct   N _____

16. Charges retorted; abusive argument   R _____

17. Reverberations   R _____

18. Grossly offensive or vulgar   S _____

19. Tending to produce sleep   S _____

20. Pale and gaunt   C _____

ANSWERS: (1) bête noire; (2) cadaverous; (3) carte blanche; (4) esoteric;
(5) forte; (6) cadaverous; (7) impasse; (8) esoteric; (9) incongruous;
(10) docile; (11) impasse; (12) bête noire; (13) stratification;
(14) moribund; (15) nebulous; (16) recriminations; (17) repercussions;
(18) scurrilous; (19) soporific; (20) cadaverous

IV

Here is another list of twenty descriptive phrases. We have shuffled the words, and again have repeated several. Follow the same procedure as in Section III.

1. Organizing into different groups   S _____

2. Confined to a particular circle   E _____

3. Permission without condition   C _____

4. Inextricable difficulty   I _____

5. Incompatible   I _____

6. On the point of dying   M _____

7. Confused and hazy   N _____

8. Vulgarly abusive   S _____

9. Sorting between low- and high-thread-count sheets
   S _____

10. Dead end   I _____

11. Ghastly   C _____

12. Bugaboo   B _____

13. Something in which one excels   F _____

14. Manageable   D _____

15. Hazy   N _____

16. Echoes   R _____
17. Producing sleep   S _____
18. Plants grouped by height   S _____
19. For a few   E _____
20. Specialty   F _____

ANSWERS: (1) stratification; (2) esoteric; (3) carte blanche; (4) impasse; (5) incongruous; (6) moribund; (7) nebulous; (8) scurrilous; (9) stratification; (10) impasse; (11) cadaverous; (12) bête noire; (13) forte; (14) docile; (15) nebulous; (16) repercussions; (17) soporific; (18) stratification; (19) esoteric; (20) forte

V

Let's try something new now, putting you more on your own. Write the word that best completes each sentence.

1. Some people think that fidelity in marriage is

   _____.

2. Knowledge of magic is highly _____.

3. If you hate cats with a passion, then cats are your

   _____.

4. A man suffering from tuberculosis may look

   _____.

5. The facts behind a politician's statements are often

   _____.

6. What is the one thing you hate or fear most? What is your particular _____?

7. After a dynamic presidential speech one often hears _____ abroad.

8. Arranging something into different groups is called

   _____.

9. When a husband and wife quarrel, they frequently indulge in bitter _____.

10. A lecturer with a monotonous voice often produces a
_____ effect.

11. Angry truck drivers frequently use _____
language.

12. What are you most skilled at? What is your special
_____?

13. The cow is a very _____ animal.

14. An awkward dancer would look _____ in the
ballet.

15. She gave her husband _____ to invite anyone he
wanted to the party.

ANSWERS: (1) moribund; (2) esoteric; (3) bête noire; (4) cadaverous;
(5) nebulous; (6) bête noire; (7) repercussions; (8) stratification;
(9) recriminations; (10) soporific; (11) scurrilous; (12) forte;
(13) docile; (14) incongruous; (15) carte blanche

VI

Your tasks are becoming more challenging with each new exercise—and
here is a particularly hard one. Write the word that is *opposite* in meaning to each of the following phrases. *Note well: Opposite, not synonymous!* Again, some will be required more than once.

1. Known to all _____

2. One big pile _____

3. In keeping with surroundings _____

4. Stimulating, like coffee _____

5. Radiantly healthy _____

6. Limited power _____

7. Crystal clear _____

8. Easy sailing _____

9. One's weak suit _____

10. Restricted power _____

11. Mutual praise _____

12. The thing you love most _____

13. Decent in expression _____

14. Something in which one is unskilled _____

15. In a healthy state _____

16. Stubborn _____

17. Not the least bit hazy _____

18. Esoteric _____

19. Keeps you awake _____

20. Grouped altogether _____

ANSWERS: (1) esoteric; (2) stratification; (3) incongruous; (4) soporific; (5) cadaverous; (6) carte blanche; (7) nebulous; (8) impasse; (9) forte; (10) carte blanche; (11) recriminations; (12) bête noire; (13) scurrilous; (14) forte; (15) moribund; (16) docile; (17) nebulous; (18) esoteric; (19) soporific; (20) stratification

VII

It is extraordinarily difficult to write the definitions of a word. And yet your understanding of a word must be somewhat nebulous if you can't define it. Try your hand at writing brief definitions of the following words:

1. *bête noire* _____

_____

2. *cadaverous* _____

_____

3. *carte blanche* _____

_____

4. *esoteric* _____

_____

5. *forte* _____

_____

6. *impasse* _____

_____

7. *incongruous* _____

_____

8. *docile* _____

_____

9. *stratification* _____

10. *moribund* _____

11. *nebulous* _____

12. *recriminations* _____

13. *repercussions* _____

_____

14. *scurrilous* _____

_____

15. *soporific* _____

_____

ANSWERS:

1. A person or object of fear or aversion; a bugbear
2. Pale, ghastly, corpselike
3. An order signed in blank; unconditional authority
4. Adapted exclusively for the initiated and enlightened few
5. Your strong point; that skill in which you excel
6. An impassable road or way; a blind alley; an insurmountable situation
7. Out of place; inharmonious
8. Easily led and managed
9. Organizing something into different groups
10. In a dying state
11. Hazy; cloudy; amorphous
12. Accusations repelled by other accusations; abusive arguments

13. Reverberations; echoes
14. Coarse, opprobrious abuse
15. Tending to cause or to produce sleep

You have learned the words in this chapter in the way that you normally learn words in your everyday life. That is, you first come across a new word in a book or in your newspaper, or you hear someone speak it. You wonder at its meaning. Your understanding of the word gradually clears, and each time you see or hear it again, you find that your knowledge of it is becoming more secure. Finally you learn to know it so well that you dare to use it in your writing and speaking. You might even be able to define it, as you have done in this chapter, if you were called upon to do so, although this is the hardest challenge of all. That is, the methods we are using in this book are the methods by which you naturally and unself-consciously learned most of the words in your vocabulary before you picked up and started working with us.

X	X	X	X	X	X	X
X	X	X	X	X	X	X
X	X	X	X	X	X	X
X	X	X	25	26	27	28
29	30					

Words That Describe You

Keep in mind this important point in reference to your vocabulary improvement program. If you can personalize your new words, if you can make them bear some relationship to yourself and your way of living, you then materially increase your chances of making these words a *permanent* part of your vocabulary.

You cannot learn words in a vacuum. That is, if a word cannot be made to have a bearing on your life, if it cannot be brought within the circle of your own thoughts, if it cannot be made a part of your own personality or of your attitudes, then that word will remain useless to you.

I

The words in this chapter should, therefore, be thought of in reference to *yourself*. Let us, for the next few pages, consider your own attitudes toward life.

1. Do you view with a certain degree of tolerance the eccentricities and foibles of other humans? Are you broadminded, sympathetic, inclined to see the other person's point of view? Do your tastes cover

a wide range? For example, in your reading, can you be interested in everything from detective stories to Russian novels? In your eating, do your likes run the gamut from a New England dinner of boiled beef to a gourmet's delight of exotic seafood? Yes? Then we will characterize you as a person whose tastes, interests, desires, and sympathies are, in one word, *catholic.*

2. Do you make trouble by your unreasoning, irascible, and vainglorious patriotism? Do you carry your jealousy of your country's honor to an absurd and ridiculous extreme? You are *chauvinistic.*

3. Are you inclined to give up the struggle before the battle is lost? Are you all too ready to lay down your arms and admit defeat at a time when braver and more optimistic souls would see many reasons for carrying on? You are a *defeatist.*

4. Do you like to dabble in the arts or the sciences? Fool a little bit with photography, only to abandon it, say, for stamp collecting? If you flit like a butterfly from interest to interest, never concentrating for any length of time on one, you are a *dilettante.*

5. Are you one whose main purpose in life seems to be the attainment of pleasure? Do you put too high a value on the luxuries of life? Are you fond of eating and drinking, and are you an expert in the choice of wines and foods? You are an *epicurean.*

6. Perhaps you find yourself in such a financial position that you must calculate closely the money costs of all your activities. Then, of course, you must practice economy. But are you *too* close-fisted with money? Do people call you stingy? You are *parsimonious.*

7. Do you look with contempt upon artists and those with an artistic temperament? Are you ignorant? Prejudiced? Blindly conventional? Narrow-minded? Do you tend to have low aims in life and are you inclined to be materialistic? You are a *philistine.*

8. Are you wasteful, extravagant, inclined to spend your money, time, energy, and talent without care or thought? You are a *profligate.*

9. Do you meet the tragedies of life with a stiff upper lip? Do you

conceal your emotions, no matter how great your mental or physical suffering may be? You are a *stoic*.

10. Finally, do you happen to know a man who is so absurdly and slavishly devoted to his wife that he is the joke of the neighborhood? He is *uxorious*.

❚❚

Now, that was a big order. Possibly many, or even all, of the words of this chapter are unfamiliar to you. If so, the exercises to come will make them your best friends. Or possibly you are well acquainted with most or all of them. In that case, the pages that follow will provide an opportunity for an even warmer and deeper intimacy.

First, of course, we pronounce them aloud—several times. As you say each one, think of, or check back on, the meaning, and decide whether the adjective or noun does, or does not, fit you personally; then check the proper box.

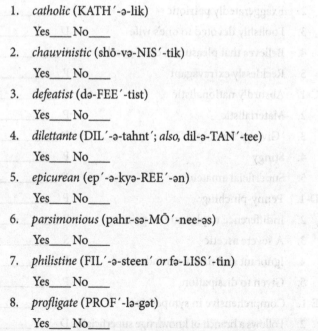

1. *catholic* (KATH´-ə-lik)
    Yes____ No____

2. *chauvinistic* (shō-və-NIS´-tik)
    Yes____ No____

3. *defeatist* (də-FEE´-tist)
    Yes____ No____

4. *dilettante* (DIL´-ə-tahnt´; *also*, dil-ə-TAN´-tee)
    Yes____ No____

5. *epicurean* (ep´-ə-kyə-REE´-ən)
    Yes____ No____

6. *parsimonious* (pahr-sə-MŌ´-nee-əs)
    Yes____ No____

7. *philistine* (FIL´-ə-steen´ *or* fə-LISS´-tin)
    Yes____ No____

8. *profligate* (PROF´-lə-gət)
    Yes____ No____

9. *stoic* (STŌ´-ik)

   Yes___ No___

10. *uxorious* (uk-SAWR´-ee-əs)

    Yes___ No___

III

To get on still better terms with these ten words, fill each one in next to its key phrase or statement. Initial letters are provided. Try not to look at Sections I or II except as a desperate last resort.

KEY		WORD
A-1.	A dabbler in art matters	D _____
2.	Unduly sparing in money	P _____
3.	Narrow-minded; uncultured	P _____
4.	Always expecting failure	D _____
5.	With liberal views and wide tastes	C _____
B-1.	Niggardly	P _____
2.	Exaggeratedly patriotic	C _____
3.	Foolishly devoted to one's wife	U _____
4.	Believes that pleasure is chief good	E _____
5.	Recklessly extravagant	P _____
C-1.	Absurdly nationalistic	C _____
2.	Materialistic	P _____
3.	"Give up the ship!"	D _____
4.	Stingy	P _____
5.	Superficial amateur	D _____
D-1.	Penny-pinching	P _____
2.	Indifference to pleasure or pain	S _____
3.	A severe ascetic	S _____
4.	Ignorant and narrow-minded	P _____
5.	Given to dissipation	P _____
E-1.	Comprehensive in sympathies	C _____
2.	Follows a branch of knowledge superficially	D _____

3. Loves the refinements of pleasure   E _____

4. Excessively patriotic   C _____

5. "Eat and be merry!"   E _____

F-1. With exquisite taste in food and drink   E _____

2. Abandoned in character and principles   P _____

3. Insensible to virtue and decency   P _____

4. Wasteful of money   P _____

5. Excessively fond of one's wife   U _____

ANSWERS: A. (1) dilettante; (2) parsimonious; (3) philistine; (4) defeatist; (5) catholic B. (1) parsimonious; (2) chauvinistic; (3) uxorious; (4) epicurean; (5) profligate C. (1) chauvinistic; (2) philistine; (3) defeatist; (4) parsimonious; (5) dilettante D. (1) parsimonious; (2) stoic; (3) stoic; (4) philistine; (5) profligate E. (1) catholic; (2) dilettante; (3) epicurean; (4) chauvinistic; (5) epicurean F. (1) epicurean; (2) profligate; (3) profligate; (4) profligate; (5) uxorious

IV

Each of the nine paragraphs that follow describes one of the words that we have been talking about. Can you tell which one and write it in?

1. My taste is highly cultivated for all things. While I am not by any means promiscuous in my interests, still I can always see the other person's point of view. I am tolerant to a great degree, for my sympathies are comprehensive and all embracing. I am _____.

2. Frugal? To the last ditch! People have even accused me of being tight-fisted and stingy, and I am afraid that if they are referring to my attitude toward spending money, they are correct. I am _____.

3. I have been accused of being without emotions, but the fact is that I have merely trained myself to be indifferent alike to pain and pleasure. I am a (an) _____.

4. I am greatly interested in the fine arts, but being a person of independent means, I don't have to really work hard at them, and it isn't necessary for me to make a living out of them. They are more or less of a pastime with me. I am a (an) _____.

5. My country? The best, the finest, the truest, the richest, the bravest, and if you don't think so you had better keep away from me. Why, I can scarcely find adjectives to describe my pride in my birthplace or to show the utter contempt I feel for all other lands. I am _____.

6. I don't think it's fair to call me a traitor to my ideals. It's just that I do not care to fight what I know to be a losing battle. I am a (an) _____.

7. Other people can waste time pampering artists and poets if they want to, but give me a businessman every time—the kind who is interested in material things like making money. And while we're on the subject, those people who keep their noses buried in books all the time and who are always worrying about knowledge and progress and liberalism? Well, I can put them also on my list of people who won't be missed! I am a (an) _____.

8. Laugh at me if you like and say that my wife uses me as a footstool. I don't care! Nothing I do will ever be good enough for her! I am _____.

9. As for me, I like my pleasure. Other people can work and slave and worry about the future and save their money, but not I! Give me a good time any day! Let the little milquetoasts keep their noses to the grindstone and lead temperate lives. I figure money is made to spend, and I believe in the old proverb "Eat, drink, and be merry." I am a (an) _____.

ANSWERS: (1) catholic; (2) parsimonious; (3) stoic; (4) dilettante; (5) chauvinistic; (6) defeatist; (7) philistine; (8) uxorious; (9) epicurean

V

By now you are developing real and assured control over these words. Therefore, you will be able to sail through the next exercise with the greatest of ease and a perfect or near-perfect score. Check *a, b,* or *c.*

1. A person of *catholic* tastes is
   a. religious.
   b. moral.
   c. sympathetic.

2. If you met an American *chauvinist* it would be safe to remark:
   a. "I would really rather live abroad."
   b. "I love my country and I despise all other nations."
   c. "Listen, America has plenty of black marks on her record! How about the Spanish-American War?"

3. The *defeatist* is a
   a. coward.
   b. pessimist.
   c. bully.

4. Anybody knows that a *dilettante* is
   a. a master of the arts.
   b. a struggling young artist.
   c. one who follows the arts as a pastime.

5. The *epicurean's* greatest delight comes from
   a. pleasure.
   b. cruelty.
   c. self-torment.

6. *Parsimonious?* He's a
   a. miser.

    b. spendthrift.

    c. philanthropist.

7. While the word *philistine* is of biblical origin, it now
    merely refers to a person who is

    a. hypocritically pious.

    b. narrow-minded; opposed to progress and learning.

    c. wealthy and hardhearted.

8. Few people realize that a *stoic* doesn't mind

    a. pleasure and pain.

    b. spending money.

    c. getting drunk.

9. An *uxorious* man

    a. foolishly and fondly dotes on his wife.

    b. is completely penniless.

    c. always complains of the way life treats him.

10. A *profligate* person is

    a. dishonest.

    b. insincere.

    c. wasteful.

ANSWERS: (1) c; (2) b; (3) b; (4) c; (5) a; (6) a; (7) b; (8) a; (9) a; (10) c

VI

And now for the acid test of your learning. Without checking back to
any previous material, can you write each word next to its definition?

1. Broad-minded in views _____

2. An exaggerated patriot _____

3. Follows the policy or practice of admitting defeat too
    quickly _____

4. One who dabbles in art and letters _____

5. One who makes a profession of pleasure. A connoisseur of
    food and wine _____

6. Unnecessarily frugal _____

7. A person with a plebeian type of mind. An individual of materialistic tastes who is interested neither in art nor letters _____

8. Completely given up to dissipation; dissolute; wasteful _____

9. A person showing no emotion over pleasure or pain _____

10. Extravagantly submissive to, and doting upon, one's wife _____

ANSWERS: (1) catholic; (2) chauvinist; (3) defeatist; (4) dilettante; (5) epicurean; (6) parsimonious; (7) philistine; (8) profligate; (9) stoic; (10) uxorious

In all likelihood this has not been an easy chapter. But it is true, isn't it, that all learning and all the skills are acquired only by dogged, systematic, and intensive work? After all, the greatest obstacle to anyone's getting ahead is just plain laziness. The average man makes a fair success with very ordinary effort, and conversely, most people lose out in life just because they won't take the trouble to win. That's why there's always so much room at the top.

If you will make use of the ideas in this book, they will open many doors to you. If you will make the precepts of this book a lifetime habit, the habit will take care of you, and lead you to greater success. Success itself is a habit.

Life has many prizes waiting for the winner. And, after all, it's a lot less exhausting to win than to worry.

X	X	X	X	X	X	X
X	X	X	X	X	X	X
X	X	X	X	X	X	X
X	X	X	X	26	27	28
29	30					

French Phrases You Can Use

The rivers of all languages have flowed into the vast reservoir of English.

The following paragraph will give you just a hint of its varied sources. Each of the italicized words came into English from a foreign language.

"The *sky* was teeming rain. The *boss* has a touch of *influenza*. He came up on the *veranda*, put down his *mammoth umbrella*, entered the comfortable *oasis* of his living room, and sat down. He filled his pipe with *tobacco*, warmed himself first with hot *cocoa*, then *coffee*, and listened to his pet *canary* sing."

Here are the parentages of these words:

sky: Old Norse
boss: Dutch
influenza: Italian
veranda: Portuguese
mammoth: Russian

umbrella: Italian

oasis: Egyptian

tobacco: West Indian

cocoa: Mexican

coffee: Arabic

canary: Spanish

The main contributors to English, however, are not the languages from which the above examples have been taken. They are, rather, French, Latin, and Greek.

French, as would be understandable, has added a large number of delicate and graceful words and phrases to our speech. Many of these have been adopted so recently that they still retain their Gallic flavor.

I

Here are ten common French importations:

1. If a prisoner of war were being tortured and were on the point of death, the final stroke that killed him would be the *coup de grâce.* Any blow that puts a suffering and greatly weakened animal, person, or institution out of its misery is a *coup de grâce.* Thus, we will say, a conqueror has allowed a subject nation to continue, for a time, with nominal independence. When and if that conqueror decides to overrun the vanquished nation and completely destroy its last vestige of freedom, he will be delivering the *coup de grâce.*

2. Anyone who is in the way, out of place, or not wanted is *de trop.* If little brother insists on sitting in the living room when his sister's beau comes a-calling, he is considered *de trop.*

3. In a sophisticated conversation, slightly off-color or improper remarks are sometimes made in terms that seem innocent. Any word or phrase that has two meanings, one of them an indelicate one, is called a *double-entendre.*

4. You are *en rapport* with someone when there is a perfect meeting of minds and a complete absence of friction.

5. A cooperative spirit on the part of a group, combined with an enthusiastic submergence of self-interest for the sake of the common good, is called *esprit de corps*. A crack regiment is sometimes famed for its *esprit de corps*.

6. Napoleon proved himself to be a leader *par excellence*. Escoffier, noted the world over for his cuisine, was a chef *par excellence*. Ralph Waldo Emerson, we might say, was the interpreter of Plato *par excellence*.

7. If your mind is perfectly attuned to your surroundings, if you are alive and alert to all that is going on around you, if you are on guard, wide awake, eager, expectant, you are on the *qui vive*.

8. A medley of things, an assorted and heterogeneous mixture of great variety, is called a *potpourri*.

9 and 10. Have you ever met a man or woman with perfect poise? Do you notice how he or she says exactly the correct and charming thing at the proper time? Never is such a person guilty of a *faux pas*, an embarrassing mistake; on the contrary, your perfectly poised, sophisticated, cosmopolitan friend is the possessor of *savoir faire*.

II

The pronunciation of words from the French does not require a Gallic accent—all have been somewhat Anglicized. When you use such a word, and we expect that you occasionally will, don't pause significantly as if you were about to break into song. On the contrary, say the Parisian import as naturally as any other word—after all, thousands upon thousands of English words come from foreign tongues: from Greek, Latin, Old Norse, German, Dutch, Italian, Portuguese, Chinese, Japanese, etc.

True, with French imports, Anglicization has not gone quite as far as with most others, so do not be surprised that the sounds you will be making will not account for all the letters in every word.

Here, then, is a close approximation of our terms from the French. Practice them carefully, aloud, and many times.

1. *coup de grâce* (koō′-də-GRAHSS′)
2. *de trop* (də-TRŌ)
3. *double-entendre* (DŌŌ′-blə-ahn-TAHN′-drə)
4. *en rapport* (ahn′-ra′-PAWR′)
5. *esprit de corps* (es-pree′-də-KAWR′)
6. *par excellence* (pahr′-ek-sə-LAHNSS′)
7. *qui vive* (kee′-VEEV′)
8. *potpourri* (pō′-pōō′-REE′)
9. *faux pas* (fō′-PAH′)
10. *savoir faire* (sav′-wahr′-FAIR′)
    (Incidentally, all ten phrases still maintain their foreign citizenship—therefore they are often underlined when written or italicized when printed.)

III

The literal translations of these ten French terms will help establish the meanings in your mind.

1. *Coup de grâce*: Blow of mercy
2. *De trop*: Too much
3. *Double-entendre*: Double meaning
4. *En rapport*: In harmonious relation
5. *Esprit de corps*: Spirit of the body
6. *Par excellence*: By excellence
7. *Qui vive*: Who lives
8. *Potpourri*: Rotten pot
9. *Faux pas*: False step
10. *Savoir faire*: To know how to do

IV

The ten words of this chapter have not yet been defined for you. Their meanings have at most been sketched in. Nevertheless a careful rereading of Section I will make it possible for you to write the correct French terms next to each of the following synonyms or synonymous phrases. Some of the terms will be called for many times in the lists that are given below.

A 1. Out of place   D _____
   2. Group enthusiasm   E _____
   3. Double meaning   D _____
   4. Surpassingly good   P _____
   5. On the alert   *on the* Q _____

B 1. In the very choicest manner   P _____
   2. In agreement   E _____
   3. In the way   D _____
   4. Mixture   P _____
   5. Decisive blow   C _____

C 1. On your toes   *on the* Q _____
   2. Two's company   D _____
   3. Finishing stroke   C _____
   4. Preeminently   P _____
   5. Off-color ambiguity   D _____

D 1. In harmonious relationship   E _____
   2. On guard   *on the* Q _____
   3. Jealous regard for the honor of the group   E _____
   4. Medley   P _____
   5. Embarrassing error   F _____

E 1. Poise   S _____
   2. Little of everything   P _____
   3. In accord   E _____
   4. Knowing and doing the graceful thing   S _____
   5. Embarrassing mistake   F _____

ANSWERS:

A. (1) *de trop*; (2) *esprit de corps*; (3) *double-entendre*;
   (4) *par excellence*; (5) *on the qui vive*

B. (1) *par excellence*; (2) *en rapport*; (3) *de trop*; (4) *potpourri*;
   (5) *coup de grâce*

C. (1) *on the qui vive*; (2) *de trop*; (3) *coup de grâce*; (4) *par excellence*;
   (5) *double-entendre*

D. (1) *en rapport*; (2) *on the qui vive*; (3) *esprit de corps*; (4) *potpourri*;
   (5) *faux pas*

E. (1) *savoir faire*; (2) *potpourri*; (3) *en rapport*; (4) *savoir faire*;
   (5) *faux pas*

V

Below you will find ten statements in which the French words and phrases we have been studying are used; some are true, others false. Write T or F next to each statement.

1. The divorce was granted to the wife, who also got custody of the children and the dog, and possession of the home, furniture, bank accounts, and both cars. On top of all this, as the *coup de grâce*, she was awarded 75 percent of her husband's salary as alimony. _____

2. Someone we enjoy being with is usually *de trop*. _____

3. Naïve girls indulge in frequent *doubles-entendres*. _____

4. A husband and wife should be *en rapport*. _____

5. A defeated army is full of *esprit de corps*. _____

6. Sarah Bernhardt was admitted to be an actress *par excellence*. _____

7. A book of famous quotations is a *potpourri* of literary gems. _____

8. A prize-fighter must be on the *qui vive* when he is in the ring. _____

9. A finishing school claims to give young girls *savoir faire.* _____

10. A *faux pas* is generally embarrassing. _____

ANSWERS: (1) T; (2) F; (3) F; (4) T; (5) F; (6) T; (7) T; (8) T; (9) T; (10) T

VI

Here, finally, is the last test of your familiarity with the French imports studied in this chapter. Without reference to previous material, fill in each term next to its definition. Can you spell them correctly?

1. The mortal stroke _____

2. Said of a person who is in the way, out of place, or not wanted _____

3. A word or phrase with double meaning _____

4. In harmonious relation one with the other _____

5. The common devotion of members to an organization _____

6. Preeminent; beyond comparison _____

7. A mixture; a medley; a mélange _____

8. The challenge of a French sentinel, meaning "Who goes there?" Hence, on the alert _____

9. The ability to say and do the right thing at the right time _____

10. A misstep; an embarrassing mistake _____

ANSWERS: (1) *coup de grâce*; (2) *de trop*; (3) *double-entendre*; (4) *en rapport*; (5) *esprit de corps*; (6) *par excellence*; (7) *potpourri*; (8) *qui vive*; (9) *savoir faire*; (10) *faux pas*

These ten phrases are only a few of the thousands of French imports that have become the adopted children of our language. Used with discretion, they can take their places as the grace notes of cultured conversation and writing. You will be surprised how many you will hear and see if you start listening and watching for them.

X̶	X̶	X̶	X̶	X̶	X̶	X̶
X̶	X̶	1̶0̶	1̶1̶	1̶2̶	1̶3̶	1̶4̶
1̶5̶	1̶6̶	1̶7̶	1̶8̶	1̶9̶	2̶0̶	2̶1̶
2̶2̶	2̶3̶	2̶4̶	2̶5̶	2̶6̶	27	28
29	30					

Words About Words

Every specialty, naturally, has its own terminology. The lawyers, the preachers, the doctors, all speak their own language. The physician, for instance, used to have to know the names of 707 different arteries, 71 bones, 79 convolutions, 433 muscles, 230 nerves, 403 veins, 295 poisons, 109 tumors, and also about 10,000 drugs . . . though those figures may have changed . . .

The philologist speaks his own language, too, and unless we were versed in his speech we would find it difficult to understand him when he talked of phonology, phonemics, and morphology.

We can, however, pick a few of the more popular words that lie in this field of language, ones that we can use in common conversation. For some of the most interesting words in our language are words about words. Here are ten such:

1. *anticlimax* (an´-tee-KLY´-max´)
2. *analogy* (a-NAL´-ə-jee)
3. *ambiguity* (am´-bə-GYOO´-ə-tee)
4. *cliché* (klee-SHAY´)

5. *epigram* (EP´-ə-gram´)
6. *euphemism* (Y$\overline{OO}$´-fə-miz´-əm)
7. *redundancy* (ree-DUN´-dən-see)
8. *non sequitur* (non-SEK´-wə-tər)
9. *persiflage* (PUR´-sə-flahzh´)
10. *simile* (SIM´-ə-lee)

I

Here is an example of each:

1. *Anticlimax*

   Dr. Jones and Dr. Smith will be guest speakers at the County Medical Society meeting Tuesday night at Mineola. Dr. Jones will take his topic from the psalm: "Behold how good and pleasant it is for brethren to dwell together in unity." Dr. Smith will speak on flat feet.

2. *Analogy*

   Your body is like a machine. Put in the proper fuel and it will function efficiently.

3. *Ambiguity*

   The farmer's helper took his car out of the garage. (Whose car did he take?)

4. *Cliché*

   "It's a great life if you don't weaken."

5. *Epigram*

   It is more blessed to give than to receive.

6. *Euphemism*

   "Mortician" or "funeral director" for *undertaker*. "Lady of the night" for *prostitute*. "Powder room" for *toilet*. "Pass away" for *die*. "Limb" for *leg*. "Derrière" or "rear" for *behind*. "Intimate relations" for *sexual intercourse*.

7. *Redundancy*

   The biggest, the greatest, the most stupendous show on earth.

8. *Non Sequitur*

   "Despite her age, her interest in music never flagged. During the past year she has crocheted a bedspread and a tablecloth."

9. *Persiflage*

   "Man never knows precisely what is right
   So, torn between a purpose and a doubt,
   He first makes windows to let in the light,
   And then hangs curtains up to shut it out."

10. *Simile*

    As thick as seagulls on a rock.

II

We have spoken before of noun endings (*-ity, -ence, -ance, -ion,* etc.), and have changed adjectives into nouns. Now, in reverse, let us change nouns into adjectives.

Some common adjective endings are *-ic* (as in *dynamic*), *-ical* (as in *biological*), *-ous* (as in *marvelous*), *-ant* and *-ent* (as in *triumphant, persistent*), *-al* (as in *banal*), and *-ive* (as in *active*).

Use your innate sense of language to change the following nouns into their adjective forms. Note also the examples of other noun-adjective transformations presented as guides, and test the sound of the form you devise in the sentence offered.

1. Change *anticlimax* to an adjective.

   (Similar transformation: *climax—climactic*)

   After the great naval victory, the sinking of a single enemy trawler was _____.

2. Change *analogy* to an adjective.

   (*bigamy—bigamous*)

   Let us discuss an _____ situation.

3. Change *ambiguity* to an adjective.

   (*superfluity—superfluous*)

   That is an _____ statement.

4. Change *epigram* to an adjective.
   (*diagram—diagrammatic*)
   Oscar Wilde has an _____ style.
5. Change *euphemism* to an adjective.
   (*antagonism—antagonistic*)
   Let us use a more _____ term.
6. Change *redundancy* to an adjective.
   (*militancy—militant*)
   Your statement is _____.

ANSWERS: (1) anticlimactic (an´-tee-kly-MAK´-tik); (2) analogous
(a-NAL´-ə-gəs); (3) ambiguous (am-BIG´-yoo-əs); (4) epigrammatic
(ep´-ə-grə-MAT´-ik); (5) euphemistic (yoo´-fə-MISS´-tik);
(6) redundant (ree-DUN´-dənt)

III

Can you write the proper term next to each definition? Initial letters are
provided to assist with your success.

1. A rhetorical figure expressing comparison or
   likeness   S _____
2. Partial agreement or resemblance between things somewhat
   different; similarity in certain aspects   A _____
3. A light, flippant style of conversation or writing; banter;
   raillery   P _____
4. A stale, worn-out, or stereotyped phrase, either written or
   spoken   C _____
5. An inference, or conclusion, that does not follow from the
   facts as stated   N _____
6. A gradual or sudden decrease in the importance or impres-
   siveness of what is said; the opposite of climax; a ludicrous or
   ridiculous drop in thought and expression, sometimes from
   the sublime to the ridiculous   A _____

7. Vagueness; indefiniteness; uncertainty; an expression whose meaning can be taken in two or more ways A _____

8. A pithy saying in prose or verse that crystallizes a wise or witty thought E _____

9. A pleasing expression used in place of one which is plainer or more accurate but which might be offensive, embarrassing, or in bad taste E _____

10. Unnecessary repetition or the employment of more words than are necessary R _____

ANSWERS: (1) simile; (2) analogy; (3) persiflage; (4) cliché; (5) non sequitur; (6) anticlimax; (7) ambiguity; (8) epigram; (9) euphemism; (10) redundancy

IV

If we trace the ancestry of words, we can often throw a new light on their meanings; also, we dramatize them and make them vivid. Here are the sources, all but one of them Latin or Greek, of the ten "words about words."

1. *Anticlimax.* Greek *anti,* "opposite to," and *klimax,* "ladder." So an *anticlimax* is really the opposite of climbing up; that is, it is climbing *down* the ladder of importance.

2. *Analogy.* Greek *ana,* "according to," plus *logos,* which we have met before with the meaning of "word" or "study." In this context, *logos* means "proportion." Things *analogous* to each other, while different, are similar in proportion.

3. *Ambiguity.* Latin *ambi,* "around," plus *agere,* "to go." When you make an *ambiguous* statement you are going around the subject!

4. *Cliché.* A French word that means "an electrotype or stereotype plate for printing." This is why a statement

of yours that is stereotyped, fixed, and lacking in originality is called a *cliché*.

5. *Epigram*. Greek *epi*, "on," and *graphein*, "write."

6. *Euphemism*. Greek *eu*, "well," and *phemi*, "speak." So if you utter a *euphemism*, you are at least making an effort to give a nice turn to a subject that would otherwise be disagreeable.

7. *Redundancy*. From the Latin *red*, "back," and *unda*, "wave." The waves are driven back on the shore and repeat themselves like your words when you are redundant.

8. *Non sequitur*. The direct translation from the Latin literally means "it does not follow."

9. *Persiflage*. From the Latin *per*, meaning "through," and *sibilare*, "to hiss" or "to whistle." Possibly, since *persiflage* sometimes means banter, there may be a significance in the fact that whistling or hissing can be sounds of derision.

10. *Simile*. From the Latin *similis*, "similar."

✗	✗	✗	✗	✗	✗	✗
✗	✗	✗	✗	✗	✗	✗
✗	✗	✗	✗	✗	✗	✗
✗	✗	✗	✗	✗	✗	28
29	30					

Word Building by the "Unfolding Process"

Let us now approach the problem of word development from a slightly different direction. We will still rely on the indirect method: that is, the method that shows you a word first in its context, rather than flashing it on you alone and away from its meaning in a sentence.

The meanings and uses of the following group of difficult words will be revealed by what we might call, for want of a better name, the "unfolding process." As you meet each word, even though it is for the first time, its meaning will be partially shown to you by the context, and its full meaning will gradually unfold before the chapter is over.

I

Read each sentence, noting particularly the italicized word and attempting some judgment of its meaning.

1. He lives a severe and *abstemious* life.
2. That is a *chimerical* and wholly unfounded fear.
3. Hunger among millions is a strange *facet* of affluent America.

4. Honesty is a *fetish* with him.

5. The *Machiavellian* moves of the crime syndicate are astounding.

6. *Ochlocracy* is sometimes a result of war.

7. Only God is truly *omniscient*.

8. When John's treachery was discovered, he truly became a *pariah*.

9. The dishonest employee received a *peremptory* dismissal.

10. The prisoner painted a *poignant* picture of his suffering.

11. The wife of Socrates was sour and *querulous*.

12. That is the most ridiculous and *specious* argument I have ever heard.

13. Fear of riots and civil disorders was *ubiquitous* in the late 1960s.

14. He is so *unctuous* I cannot bear him.

15. That *vainglorious* and pompous senator annoys all who know him.

II

Now say the words aloud.

1. *abstemious* (ab-STEE´-mee-əs)

2. *chimerical* (kə-MAIR´-ə-kəl)

3. *facet* (FASS´-ət)

4. *fetish* (FET´-ish *or* FEE´-tish)

5. *Machiavellian* (mak´-ee-ə-VEL´-ee-ən)

6. *ochlocracy* (ok-LOK´-rə-see)

7. *omniscient* (om-NISH´-ənt)

8. *pariah* (pə-RY´-ə)

9. *peremptory* (pə-REMP´-tə-ree)

10. *poignant* (POIN´-yənt *or* POIN´-ənt)

11. *querulous* (KWAIR´-ə-ləs)

12. *specious* (SPEE´-shəs)
13. *ubiquitous* (yōō-BIK´-wə-təs)
14. *unctuous* (UNK´-chōō-əs)
15. *vainglorious* (vain-GLAW´-ree-əs)

III

Feel free to refer to the sentences in Section I as you check what you think is the correct synonym or synonymous phrase for each word.

1. *abstemious*
   a. licentious
   b. miserly
   c. sparing in the use of food and drink
2. *chimerical*
   a. foolish
   b. fanciful
   c. difficult
3. *facet*
   a. side; aspect
   b. tap
   c. failure
4. *fetish*
   a. shoe
   b. object of worship
   c. love
5. *Machiavellian*
   a. kingly
   b. politically cunning
   c. angelic
6. *ochlocracy*
   a. dictatorship
   b. mob rule
   c. democracy

7. *omniscient*
   a. omnipotent
   b. rare
   c. all-knowing

8. *pariah*
   a. outcast
   b. madman
   c. expatriate

9. *peremptory*
   a. tardy
   b. fearful
   c. decisive and final

10. *poignant*
    a. piquant
    b. painfully moving
    c. bitter

11. *querulous*
    a. questioning
    b. complaining; fretful
    c. angry

12. *specious*
    a. remarkable
    b. cunning
    c. subtly false

13. *ubiquitous*
    a. ecstatic
    b. found, or existing, everywhere
    c. pestiferous

14. *unctuous*
    a. dirty
    b. unconcerned

    c.   bland and smugly smooth in pretense of concern, sincerity, or spirituality

15. *vainglorious*

    a.   silly

    b.   boastful

    c.   fastidious

ANSWERS: (1) c; (2) b; (3) a; (4) b; (5) b; (6) b; (7) c; (8) a; (9) c; (10) b; (11) b; (12) c; (13) b; (14) c; (15) b

IV

Gradually, as these words "unfold" for you, you will begin to feel more and more power over them. You met each word in context; next, you heard the word in your own voice and felt comfortable with the sound of it; then you picked a synonym out of three choices. With each exercise you gained a little more self-confidence.

The next step is to see if you can think of the word when the initial letter and a synonym or brief definition are given. This exercise checks your understanding, your power of recall, and your spelling.

1. Final, brooking no opposition or argument; hence, decisive to the point of being dictatorial   P _____

2. Mob rule   O _____

3. Outcast   P _____

4. Shrewdly cunning; politically devious   M _____

5. All-knowing   O _____

6. Object of worship   F _____

7. Sharply affecting the feelings; touching   P _____

8. Found everywhere   U _____

9. One side, face, or aspect of something   F _____

10. Complaining; whining; showing discontent   Q _____

11. Very moderate, almost austere, in one's habits of eating and drinking   A _____

12. Seemingly true, but actually false S _____

13. Boastfully conceited and self-important V _____

14. Absurdly fanciful or unreal C _____

15. Smooth and ingratiating, but obviously insincere, in one's pretense of piety, spirituality, concern, or earnestness
    U _____

ANSWERS: (1) peremptory; (2) ochlocracy; (3) pariah;
(4) Machiavellian; (5) omniscient; (6) fetish; (7) poignant;
(8) ubiquitous; (9) facet; (10) querulous; (11) abstemious;
(12) specious; (13) vainglorious; (14) chimerical; (15) unctuous

V

Now, without an initial letter to guide your thinking, can you write the word that each phrase or sentence hints at?

1. Reign of terror during French Revolution _____

2. An object of worship among savages _____

3. An absurd creation of the imagination _____

4. A leper _____

5. Political maneuvers of dictators of the 1930s and 1940s _____

6. Arguments of a demagogue _____

7. The ice-cream vendor and his little truck on summer afternoons _____

8. The sadness of unrequited love _____

9. Boastfulness was a characteristic of Napoleon _____

10. A complaining spouse _____

11. Someone who is on a reducing diet _____

12. A diamond _____

13. God _____

14. A martinet's order to an underling _____

15. A smooth appearance of sanctity _____

ANSWERS: (1) ochlocracy; (2) fetish; (3) chimerical; (4) pariah;
(5) Machiavellian; (6) specious; (7) ubiquitous; (8) poignant;
(9) vainglorious; (10) querulous; (11) abstemious; (12) facet;
(13) omniscient; (14) peremptory; (15) unctuous

VI

"Toujours la pratique," say the French—"Always the practice." We enlarge
your opportunities for practice by offering you four groups of five sentences, each sentence to be completed by one of the fifteen words. Answers follow each group so you can check your results as you go along.
Some of the words may be called for more than once.

GROUP 1

1. The speaker painted a _____ picture of hunger in America.

2. You may insist that everybody hates you and avoids
   you, but I assure you that's a _____ of your
   diseased imagination.

3. That teacher makes a _____ of discipline.

4. He is a glib, _____ person; I do not trust him.

5. Your _____ schemes to win the nomination will
   get you nowhere; already your name is anathema to
   most of your constituents.

ANSWERS: (1) poignant; (2) chimera; (3) fetish; (4) unctuous;
(5) Machiavellian

GROUP 2

1. At Christmas time the _____ holiday carol
   singers remind the public of the jolly spirits of the
   season—whether they want to remember or not.

2. That is a _____ argument, but possibly you may
   get a number of unthinking people to believe it.

3. No one can call you modest or diffident; indeed, on the
   contrary, you are the most _____ man I know.

4. Invalids, discontented wives, rejected lovers, whiny children—all these tend to be _____.

5. There are so many _____ to the international situation that it is difficult to guess what the future holds.

ANSWERS: (1) ubiquitous; (2) specious; (3) vainglorious; (4) querulous; (5) facets

GROUP 3

1. No one knows what is going to happen in the world. Things are in such an imbroglio. One would have to be _____ to know.

2. Poor people, through lack of money, are forced to be _____.

3. Looting is an excellent example of _____.

4. Sometimes it is necessary for an author to know what is going on in the minds of his characters. This is called _____.

5. After murdering Lincoln, John Wilkes Booth became a _____.

ANSWERS: (1) omniscient; (2) abstemious; (3) ochlocracy; (4) omniscience; (5) pariah

GROUP 4

1. Some mothers make their commands so _____ that they antagonize their children.

2. He is winning you over to his side with _____ reasoning.

3. His _____ machinations make him the most feared and the least trusted man in America.

4. In the spring the color green may be said to be almost _____.

5. Some housewives make an absolute _____ out of neatness.

ANSWERS: (1) peremptory; (2) specious; (3) Machiavellian; (4) ubiquitous; (5) fetish

VII

Now we are going to ask you to think *in reverse,* for the more angles from which we approach these words, the more the words will become meaningful and useful to you.

Can you figure out which of the fifteen words is *opposite in meaning* to each of the following?

1. Gluttonish _____
2. Real; in actual existence _____
3. Object of hatred _____
4. Politically direct and honest _____
5. Control over the mob so that it is without power _____
6. Completely ignorant; knowing nothing _____
7. An idol, loved by all _____
8. Indecisive; wavering _____
9. Leaving the emotions unaffected _____
10. Satisfied; uncomplaining _____
11. Authentic; true in every way _____
12. Found nowhere; completely absent _____
13. Crude and boorish _____
14. Modest _____

ANSWERS: (1) abstemious; (2) chimerical; (3) fetish; (4) Machiavellian; (5) ochlocracy; (6) omniscient; (7) pariah; (8) peremptory; (9) poignant; (10) querulous; (11) specious; (12) ubiquitous; (13) unctuous; (14) vainglorious

VIII

The defining of any word is incredibly hard. Just think, for instance, of writing a definition of "blue" in such a way that a blind man will get a clear idea of what you mean. But your very attempt to define the fifteen words we have been working with will force you to think intensively about them and will clinch their meanings for you in a way that nothing else possibly could.

When you check with the answers, you cannot expect your language to be the same as that in the definitions given; but if you find that you have covered substantially the same points, you will have proof that you have mastered the fifteen words of this chapter.

1. *absteminous:* _____

_____

_____

_____

2. *chimerical:* _____

_____

_____

_____

3. *facet:* _____

_____

_____

_____

4. *fetish:* _____

_____

_____

_____

5. *Machiavellian:* _____

_____

_____

_____

6. *ochlocracy:* _____

_____

_____

7. *omniscient:* _____

   _____

   _____

   _____

8. *pariah:* _____

   _____

   _____

   _____

9. *peremptory:* _____

   _____

   _____

   _____

10. *poignant:* _____

    _____

    _____

    _____

11. *querulous:* _____

    _____

    _____

    _____

12. *specious:* _____

    _____

    _____

    _____

13. *ubiquitous:* _____

    _____

    _____

    _____

14. *unctuous:* _____

    _____

    _____

15. *vainglorious:* _____

_____

_____

_____

ANSWERS:

1. Eating and drinking sparingly; self-denying in the indulgence of the appetites
2. Merely imaginary; fanciful; fantastic; visionary
3. One of the small surfaces cut upon a diamond or other gem. By extension, a part, aspect, or point of view
4. A material object believed to be the dwelling of a spirit that will protect the owner from harm; hence, any object of devotion or blind affection
5. Of or pertaining to the Florentine politician Niccolò Machiavelli, or to a system of political trickery
6. Mob rule
7. All-knowing, or all-wise
8. A social outcast
9. Unpleasantly positive in judgment or opinion; dogmatic; dictatorial
10. Strongly affecting the emotions; touching
11. Disposed to complain or be fretful
12. Falsely appearing right and true; seemingly plausible
13. Seeming to be everywhere at once; omnipresent
14. Smooth and bland, but insincere, in pretense of feeling, piety, spirituality, goodness, etc.
15. Excessively proud of one's attainments, accomplishments, or performance, as shown in undue elation, boasting, or self-praise.

This chapter has contained a few long and somewhat unusual words, and this leads us to a warning that we can't repeat too often. When we speak of the value of a large vocabulary, we don't mean a vocabulary of *large* words. A large word has its place. Sometimes it will crystallize a meaning that otherwise might require a whole phrase to express. Fine. Use such a word then. It will make for brevity and clarity. It is much simpler to describe a man as a "monogamist" than to have to say that "he is the type of man who believes in marrying only one wife." But never use a long word when a short one will do. Never try for fancy phrases. Persons who do that are not being "literary." They are merely being stuffy and are attempting to parade their knowledge. Don't say, "I *reside* in my *domicile*." Say, "I *live* in my *house*." You don't *commence*; you *begin*. You don't *pass away*, or *go to your reward*; you *die*. A *conflagration* is a *fire*. And you don't *retire*; you just plain *go to bed*.

The highest art is usually the simplest in form, be it sculpture or music or architecture or painting—or language.

Words from Classic Roots

We Americans are the most inventive people in the world, and we have been applying this genius continually to our language. We have been inventing words ever since the Pilgrims drew lots for land and began identifying a piece of ground as a "lot."

We have not only invented words, but, as has been indicated in this book, we have hungrily adopted them from other languages and have adapted the imported and foreign words to our own uses.

In this chapter we will explore several roads that branch off from the simple numbers *one*, *two*, and *three*. You may find that we will repeat some etymological roots that we have already had.

The Greek word *monos*, "one," appears in English words as *mono* or *mon*. Thus a *monocle* is a glass for one eye. *Monogamy* is one marriage. A *monogram* is a combination of two or more letters so arranged as to represent a single unit.

I

Can you think of some words beginning with *mono* or *mon*? The definitions should help you, but if you're stuck, check with the answers below.

1. _____ A treatise on one subject
2. _____ A speech uttered by one person
3. _____ Mental derangement confined to one idea
4. _____ An airplane with one pair of wings
5. _____ Exclusive possession or control of any one thing
6. _____ A word of one syllable
7. _____ Belief in one god
8. _____ One unvarying tone
9. _____ Government in the hands of one ruler
10. _____ Place in which a person lives alone (as one, by himself) under religious vows
11. _____ The inhabitant of the place described in item 10
12. _____ Continuing in one unvarying way or tone; hence, tiresome, dull

ANSWERS: (1) monograph; (2) monologue; (3) monomania; (4) monoplane; (5) monopoly; (6) monosyllable; (7) monotheism; (8) monotone; (9) monarchy; (10) monastery; (11) monk; (12) monotonous

If we analyze some of the words in the previous exercise, we discover a number of new roots.

1. In *monograph* we have Greek *graphein*, "to write," a root that appears in English words as *graph* or *gram*. For example:

   graphic—written; hence, vivid

   graphite—writing material

   autograph—one's name written by oneself

   chirography—handwriting

   telegram—writing from a distance

2. In *monologue* we have Greek *logos* (discussed in Chapter 13), a root with a number of different meanings—"word," "study," "science," "proportion," or "discourse." We have already learned *entomology, philology, embryology, etymology.* Others are:

   dialogue—discourse by two people

   eulogy—good words

   biology—science or study of life

   trilogy—discourse in three parts

3. *Monomania* reminds us of other words containing *mania,* "derangement":

   dipsomania—kleptomania—pyromania— nymphomania—megalomania

4. *Monotheism,* containing Greek *theos,* "god," brings to mind other words with this root:

   polytheism—theology—theocracy—atheism

II

Bi- is a prefix from Latin *bis,* "twice" or "two." Thus, *biannual,* twice a year; *bicameral,* with two houses, as the Senate and the House of Representatives in our Congress, or the House of Lords and the House of Commons in England; *biceps,* a muscle having two heads of origin; *bicuspid,* a tooth ending in two points. Can you think of other words with the prefix *bi-?*

1. _____ A vehicle with two wheels

2. _____ Occurring every two years

3. _____ Eyeglasses having two kinds of lenses

4. _____ Second marriage while the first is still in effect

5. _____ Every two months

6. _____ Something used for two eyes

7. _____ An animal with two feet

8. _____ Something cooked twice; i.e., a cracker

9. _____ Cut into two parts

10. _____ A marine animal with two shells, as an oyster, clam, etc.

ANSWERS: (1) bicycle; (2) biennial; (3) bifocals; (4) bigamy; (5) bimonthly; (6) binoculars; (7) biped; (8) biscuit; (9) bisect; (10) bivalve

If we analyze the words in the previous exercise, we can find in them some useful roots.

1. The last part of *bicycle* is from the Greek *kyklos,* "wheel" or "circle," a root found also in *cyclic, unicycle, tricycle.*

2. In *bigamy,* we have the Greek *gamos,* a root we have already learned, and the ending of *monogamy, polygamy, misogamy.*

3. *Binoculars* contains the Latin *oculus,* "eye," from which root we derive *monocle, oculist, ocular.*

4. In *biped* there is the Latin root *pedis,* "foot," also found in *pedestrian, pedal, quadruped, impede,* and *expedition.*

5. The second root in *bisect* is the Latin *sectus,* "cut," from which we also derive *section, sect, insect, intersect, trisect,* etc.

III

Tri- is a Latin or Greek prefix meaning "three." Thus, in music, a *triad* is a chord of three notes; a *triangle* is a figure of three angles; a *tricolor* is a flag of three colors. Now fill in the twelve spaces with the proper words made up of *tri:*

1. _____ A vehicle of three wheels

2. _____ Having three sides

3. _____ Made up of, or pertaining to, three languages

4. _____ A series of three literary or musical compositions

5. _____ Every three months

6. _____ The union of three persons, as the Father, the Son, and the Holy Ghost

7. _____ Three people who sing a song
8. _____ Consisting of three
9. _____ Three children born simultaneously from the same mother
10. _____ A three-legged stand, as for a camera

ANSWERS: (1) tricycle; (2) trilateral; (3) trilingual; (4) trilogy; (5) trimonthly; (6) trinity; (7) trio; (8) triple; (9) triplets; (10) tripod

Trilateral contains the Latin *lateris,* "side," found also in *bilateral,* two-sided; *quadrilateral,* four-sided; *unilateral,* one-sided; and *lateral,* pertaining to a side.

Tripod combines *tri-* with the Greek *podos,* "foot," found also in *podium,* the small raised platform on which the conductor of an orchestra stands; *chiropodist* or *podiatrist,* foot doctor; and *monopode,* a mythical single-footed creature.

IV

Are your classical (i.e., Latin and Greek) roots under control? Then, without checking with previous material, fill in two English words based on each of the roots below.

1. *monos,* "one"
   a. _____
   b. _____
2. *graphein,* "write"
   a. _____
   b. _____
3. *logos,* "word," "study," etc.
   a. _____
   b. _____
4. *mania,* "derangement"
   a. _____
   b. _____

5. *theos,* "god"

   a. _____

   b. _____

6. *bis,* "twice," "two"

   a. _____

   b. _____

7. *kyklos,* "wheel"

   a. _____

   b. _____

8. *gamos,* "marriage"

   a. _____

   b. _____

9. *oculus,* "eye"

   a. _____

   b. _____

10. *pedis,* "foot"

    a. _____

    b. _____

11. *sectus,* "cut"

    a. _____

    b. _____

12. *tri,* "three"

    a. _____

    b. _____

13. *lateris,* "side"

    a. _____

    b. _____

14. *podos,* "foot"

    a. _____

    b. _____

1	2	3	4	5	6	7
8	9	10	11	12	13	14
15	16	17	18	19	20	21
22	23	24	25	26	27	28
29	30					

Words Change Their Meanings

You may remember the anecdote that was told of King George the First of England and Sir Christopher Wren, the architect of St. Paul's Cathedral in London. Upon the completion of the masterly edifice, the king told Wren that his work was "amusing, awful, and artificial." Sir Christopher was delighted with the royal compliment, inasmuch as three hundred years ago *amusing* meant "amazing," *awful* meant "awe-inspiring," and *artificial* meant "artistic."

That is a dramatic indication of how the meanings of words change over the years. Latin and Greek, of course, are dead languages and are therefore static, but a language as vital and alive as English is in a constant state of flux.

In very olden days, roses used to "stink." This was not the fault of the flowers but of the word. In Old English "stink," and "stench" too, referred to any odor at all, good or bad. But since unpleasant odors make a stronger impression on us than others, and are, therefore, more often commented upon, the meaning of the word gradually shifted, and came finally to have only an unpleasant significance.

Similar shifts in meaning are occurring right under our eyes today. The words *smell* and *odor,* when they are unqualified by adjectives, are beginning to gather about them disagreeable connotations. The phrases "what a smell" or "what an odor" certainly no longer refer to anything pleasant. Nowadays when our noses are pleased we have to resort to such terms as *scent* and *aroma.* If these words become soiled someday, as they almost surely will, we may find ourselves resorting to *bouquet,* a word now largely restricted to the distinctive aroma of wine.

Villain is another once respectable word that degenerated. Originally a "villain" was a farm laborer, or one who worked in a villa. Some philologists think the word was helped in its downward path by its supposed connection with the unrelated word *vile.* Likewise, *hussy* is merely a contraction of the innocent word "housewife."

"Starve" used to mean "die." "Zest" was a piece of lemon peel. "Meat" in Anglo-Saxon was any food at all, as in the biblical "If meat maketh my brother to offend. . . ." In the sixteenth century *specious* meant "beautiful," *stupid* meant "amazed," and *mortified* meant "deadened." And when the American settlers founded Plymouth, *naughty* still meant just what it sounds like—"good for naught"—and in the records of the colony we find the odd phrase "small and naughty canoes."

Change is of course one of the most reliable indications of a healthy and growing language. And no language has ever grown so luxuriantly or changed so radically as English, or its close cousin, our American language. It is changing day by day.

English, like time, marches on. What a word meant yesterday it no longer means today. The word *humor* formerly referred to one's disposition or state of mind, and still more formerly, to one of the four fluids of the body, and *still* more formerly, to moisture or vapor. Now it identifies that sense by aid of which we can appreciate something funny; and *funny,* which once meant "laughable," now often means "strange or odd."

In the old days when we said a person was lying "prone," we meant, quite correctly, that he was lying on his face. Today, judging by newspaper photographs, he is usually lying on his back. In our present times a "fight" is often simply an argument; a "celebrity" is anyone who was in yesterday's gossip column. Today one can "climb up" as well as down; *lay* means "lie"; and *quite,* formerly meaning "wholly," now, like *awfully,* often means only "very." *Acclimate* has changed its pronunciation as well as its meaning, and is now usually used to show adjustment not only to weather or physical conditions, but even to one's friends. *Asylum,* which comes from the Greek *asylon,* "no right of seizure," meant originally "a place of refuge." In modern times this word has been so corrupted that it has connotations suggesting a psychiatric institution.

So our language shifts, changes, grows, and is alive to the fingertips. There are new words for new times. If conditions today were identical with those of one hundred years ago, a "cabriolet" would still mean a "light, one-horse, two-seated carriage" as it did to our great-grandfathers, and not, as it did in the 1940s, a convertible coupé. (And today, of course, since language always becomes simpler, we call it, compactly, a "convertible.")

If civilization had not changed from Anglo-Saxon times, *curious* would still mean "careful," and *silly* would still mean "blessed."

Language changes, change is normal, and one hundred years from now many of the words whose meanings are suitable to the civilization of the twenty-first century will probably undergo startling changes in order to adapt to the twenty-second.

You have come now to the end of your course. The next chapter will be a review test. You will have some idea of the progress you have made when we tell you that in these lessons you have added more words to your vocabulary than the average adult adds in ten to fifteen years. After the middle twenties, one's vocabulary growth virtually ceases unless a planned effort is made.

Remember how limited most of us are as to words. Nine native words, such as *it* and *the,* make up one-quarter of our conversation. Add thirty-four more and you have half the words of our daily speech. That is, forty-three words do 50 percent of our conversational work. There is so little you have to do to beat this average.

Write it large in your mind that a mastery of words is one of the essentials for success in every sphere of life.

Your 30-Day Vocabulary Test

You have now added the greater part of five hundred usable and valuable words to your working vocabulary. It will be interesting to find out how many of them you are still sure of.

I

Check the word or phrase closest in meaning to each italicized word.

1. *gregarious*   a. home-loving   b. party-loving   c. food-loving
2. *wanton*   a. unrestrained   b. desirous   c. useful
3. *pander*   a. fry   b. cater to   c. raise
4. *effete*   a. worn out   b. strong   c. happy
5. *vicarious*   a. actual   b. second-hand   c. vicious

II

Write five words ending in *-mania.*

1. _____
2. _____
3. _____

4. _____
5. _____

III

Write the verb, beginning with the initial letter indicated, that suits each definition.

1. To spend time in the country   R _____
2. To delay   P _____
3. To show disapproval   D _____
4. To exclude from social privileges   O _____
5. To be bright and witty   S _____

IV

Write the title of the doctor you would see for each of these troubles.

1. Eye diseases   O _____
2. Children's disease   P _____
3. Mental disorder   P _____
4. Skin trouble   D _____
5. Crooked teeth   O _____

V

What is the specialty of each of the following?

1. *Podiatrist* _____
2. *Gynecologist* _____
3. *Dermatologist* _____
4. *Oculist* _____
5. *Obstetrician* _____

VI

Check the word or phrase closest in meaning to each italicized word.

1. *panacea*   a. theory   b. information   c. cure-all
2. *vindictive*   a. revengeful   b. releasing   c. wise

3. *maudlin*   a. tearfully sentimental   b. angry   c. happy
4. *misogynist*   a. man-hater   b. marriage-hater
    c. woman-hater
5. *vitriolic*   a. glassy   b. caustic   c. mild

VII

What philosophy is implied by each of the following:

1. "There is no God."   A _____
2. "No one knows whether God exists."   A _____
3. "All virtue consists in self-interest."   E _____
4. "Pleasure is the ultimate good."   E _____
5. "My country (religion, city, etc.) is superior to all others."
    C _____

VIII

Name the field each scientist specializes in.

1. *anthropologist* _____
2. *geologist* _____
3. *archaeologist* _____
4. *embryologist* _____
5. *entomologist* _____
6. *ethnologist* _____
7. *etymologist* _____
8. *ornithologist* _____
9. *philologist* _____
10. *psychologist* _____

IX

Write the verb, beginning with the letter indicated, that fits each definition.

1. charge to   I _____
2. atone for   E _____

3. stagnate   V _____
4. cheat   M _____
5. beg   I _____

X

Check the correct definition.

1. *facilitate*   a. make better   b. make easier   c. make happier
2. *emulate*   a. imitate   b. deny   c. question
3. *gesticulate*   a. use gestures   b. use words   c. use sounds
4. *plagiarize*   a. steal literary property   b. torture   c. attack
5. *patronize*   a. cater to with condescension   b. defer to with respect   c. cater to with hesitation

XI

Write the meaning of the root and one English word built on it.

ROOT	MEANING	EXAMPLE
1. *monos*	_____	_____
2. *graphein*	_____	_____
3. *theos*	_____	_____
4. *bis*	_____	_____
5. *tri*	_____	_____

XII

Write the word that fits each definition.

1. Pathologic incendiarism   P _____
2. Fear of closed spaces   C _____
3. Sleepwalking   S _____
4. Hostility to father, with undue attachment to mother   O _____
5. Delusions of persecution   P _____

XIII

Check the proper word.

1. *Loss of memory*   a. insomnia   b. somnambulism
   c. amnesia

2. *Incessant drunkenness*   a. pyromania   b. kleptomania
   c. dipsomania

3. *Trouble with imaginary ills*   a. claustrophobia
   b. acrophobia   c. hypochondria

4. *Delight in inflicting pain on another*   a. sadism
   b. cynicism   c. iconoclasm

5. *Pandering to the passions of people to gain political power*
   a. anarchism   b. jingoism   c. demagoguery

XIV

Match the two columns by placing the appropriate letter of column B next to each word in column A. We have added an extra word in column B to make it more difficult.

A.		B.
1. disciplinarian _____		a. *coquette*
2. boot-licker _____		b. *egotist*
3. beginner _____		c. *martinet*
4. conceited fellow _____		d. *sycophant*
5. flirt _____		e. *atheist*
		f. *tyro*

XV

Proceed as before.

A.		B.
1. coin collector _____		a. *virtuoso*
2. one with good taste in food _____		b. *philologist*
3. beauty worshiper _____		c. *philatelist*

4. student of language _____   d. *numismatist*

5. skilled artist _____   e. *gourmet*

f. *esthete*

XVI

Proceed as before.

A.   B.

1. man with one wife _____   a. *ornithologist*

2. seer _____   b. *ethnologist*

3. eye doctor _____   c. *clairvoyant*

4. dabbler in art _____   d. *oculist*

5. student of birds _____   e. *monogamist*

f. *dilettante*

XVII

Write the word that fits each definition.

1. drowsiness or indifference L _____

2. full to repletion S _____

3. exhausted E _____

4. boredom E _____

5. haughtily contemptuous S _____

XVIII

Write the meaning of the root and one English word built on it.

ROOT	MEANING	EXAMPLE
1. *anthropos*	_____	_____
2. *polys*	_____	_____
3. *philein*	_____	_____
4. *misein*	_____	_____
5. *pedis*	_____	_____

XIX

Match the two columns.

A.		B.
1.	*taciturn*	a. learned
2.	*esthetic*	b. tireless
3.	*loquacious*	c. satisfyingly beautiful
4.	*indefatigable*	d. talkative
5.	*erudite*	e. silent

XX

Write the word whose meaning and initial letter are given.

1. Minor indiscretion   P _____
2. Boastfulness   B _____
3. Complicated and embarrassing situation   I _____
4. Warmongering   J _____
5. To shirk work by pretending illness   M _____

XXI

Match the two columns.

A.		B.
1.	introvert	a. truculent
2.	inhibited	b. one whose mind is turned inward
3.	diffident	c. quixotic
4.	with impractical ideals	d. shy
5.	overbearing	e. restrained

XXII

Check in each case the word *opposite* to the italicized word. Repeat: *opposite*, or *antonymous*.

1. *plebeian*   a. common   b. ordinary   c. distinguished
2. *inane*   a. wise   b. necessary   c. useful

3. *wanton* a. hopeful b. restrained c. lovely
4. *obsequious* a. brusque b. happy c. sad
5. *crass* a. rapid b. refined c. good

XXIII

Match the words of similar meaning in these two columns:

A.		B.
1.	carelessly	a. *adroitly*
2.	skillfully	b. *vociferously*
3.	sourly	c. *irascibly*
4.	smoothly	d. *glibly*
5.	loudly	e. *cursorily*

XXIV

Choose from the following lettered list a word or phrase *opposite*—repeat, *opposite*—to each numbered word below the list. Write the appropriate letter next to each number.

a. useless
b. known to all
c. disordered
d. solid
e. satisfactory
f. healthy
g. wasteful
h. necessary
i. stingy
j. wavering
k. respectful

1. *stratification*
2. *esoteric*
3. *nebulous*

4. *moribund*

5. *scurrilous*

XXV

Choose from the following lettered list a word or phrase *similar*—repeat, *similar*—in meaning to each numbered word below the list. Write the appropriate letter next to each number.

a. imaginary

b. hater of women

c. excessively fond of one's wife

d. stingy

e. overpatriotic

f. liberal

g. wasteful

h. homesickness

i. object of hatred

j. desirable

k. tireless

l. well-meaning

1. *parsimonious*

2. *catholic*

3. *uxorious*

4. *profligate*

5. *chauvinistic*

XXVI

Write "same" if the two words in a pair have similar meanings; "opposite" if they have opposing meanings.

1. *analogous*—similar _____

2. *ambiguous*—clear _____

3. *epigrammatic*—pointless _____

4. *euphemistic*—crude _____

5. *redundant*—repetitious _____

XXVII

Write the meaning of the italicized portion of each word.

1. dipso*mania* _____

2. *bi*ped _____

3. *tri*pod _____

4. *pod*ium _____

5. bi*cycle* _____

XXVIII

Proceed as before.

1. *anim*ate _____

2. bene*fit* _____

3. *fact*ory _____

4. *dict*ate _____

5. *un*ite _____

XXIX

Each one of the following five words is followed by a definition. Where the definition is correct, write "yes"; where it is incorrect write "no."

1. *ochlocracy* _____ rule by a dictator

2. *omniscient* _____ all-knowing

3. *fetish* _____ object of hate

4. *facet* _____ hope

5. *abstemious* _____ gluttonish

XXX

Write "true" or "false" next to each statement.

1. *Chimerical* things are tangible. _____

2. *Machiavellian* people are naïve. _____

3. *Pariahs* are popular. _____
4. *Diffident* people are generally *peremptory.* _____
5. *Querulous* wives are happy. _____

Allowing two points for each correct answer to the 155 items in the test you have just taken, it is possible to make a maximum score of 310. After checking with the answers below, read the results of your learning from the following table:

250–310	Excellent
200–250	Good
100–200	Fair
0–100	Poor

ANSWERS:

I. (1) b; (2) a; (3) b; (4) a; (5) b

II. dipsomania, megalomania, pyromania, kleptomania, bibliomania, egomania, nymphomania, Anglomania, Francomania, etc.

III. (1) rusticate; (2) procrastinate; (3) deprecate; (4) ostracize; (5) scintillate

IV. (1) oculist or ophthalmologist; (2) pediatrician; (3) psychiatrist; (4) dermatologist; (5) orthodontist

V. (1) feet; (2) women's diseases; (3) skin diseases; (4) eye diseases; (5) delivery of babies

VI. (1) c; (2) a; (3) a; (4) c; (5) b

VII. (1) atheism; (2) agnosticism; (3) egoism; (4) epicureanism; (5) chauvinism

VIII. (1) history of mankind; (2) rocks; (3) ancient relics or excavations; (4) unborn animals or children; (5) insects; (6) history of races; (7) derivation of words; (8) birds; (9) language; (10) human mind

IX. (1) impute; (2) expiate; (3) vegetate; (4) mulct; (5) importune

X. (1) b; (2) a; (3) a; (4) a; (5) a

XI. (1) one (monocle, monogram, monologue, monomania, monogamy, monotheism, monopode, monastery, monk, monopoly, monograph, etc.); (2) write (graphology, autograph, graphic, monograph, chirography, etc.); (3) god (theology, theocracy, monotheism, atheism, pantheism, theism, etc.); (4) twice, two (biped, bicycle, bicuspid, bilateral, binoculars, bigamy, bisect, etc.); (5) three (triangle, tricycle, tripod, trio, trinity, tricuspid, trisect, etc.)

XII. (1) pyromania; (2) claustrophobia; (3) somnambulism; (4) Oedipus complex; (5) paranoia

XIII. (1) c; (2) c; (3) c; (4) a; (5) c

XIV. (1) c; (2) d; (3) f; (4) b; (5) a

XV. (1) d; (2) e; (3) f; (4) b; (5) a

XVI. (1) e; (2) c; (3) d; (4) f; (5) a

XVII. (1) lethargy; (2) satiated; (3) enervated; (4) ennui; (5) supercilious

XVIII. (1) man, mankind (anthropology, anthropoid, misanthropy, philanthropy, etc.); (2) many (polygamy, polygon, polytechnic, polymer, polyester resin, polytheism, etc.); (3) love (philanthropy,

Philadelphia, philately, philtre, philosophy, bibliophile, Anglophile, Francophile, Russophile, philodendron, philoprogenitive, etc.); (4) hate (misanthropy, misogamy, misogyny, etc.); (5) foot (pedestrian, pedal, pedometer, impede, expedite, expedition, impediment, etc.)

XIX. (1) e; (2) c; (3) d; (4) b; (5) a

XX. (1) peccadillo; (2) braggadocio; (3) imbroglio; (4) jingoism; (5) malinger

XXI. (1) b; (2) e; (3) d; (4) c; (5) a

XXII. (1) c; (2) a; (3) b; (4) a; (5) b

XXIII. (1) e; (2) a; (3) c; (4) d; (5) b

XXIV. (1) c; (2) b; (3) d; (4) f; (5) k

XXV. (1) d; (2) f; (3) c; (4) g; (5) e

XXVI. (1) same; (2) opposite; (3) opposite; (4) opposite; (5) same

XXVII. (1) derangement; (2) twice, two; (3) three; (4) foot; (5) wheel

XXVIII. (1) mind or spirit; (2) well; (3) do, make; (4) say, tell; (5) one

XXIX. (1) no; (2) yes; (3) no; (4) no; (5) no

XXX. (1) false; (2) false; (3) false; (4) false; (5) false

One Last Word:
A Lifetime Habit

In one sense you have finished this book. In another we hope that you have just begun.

You have, perhaps, learned to know many words more intimately. And *any* new word that you learn in your life will add amazingly to your power to think. Once a person thinks—really thinks—they have little competition. You may remember that the Irish playwright George Bernard Shaw one time said that few people think more than two or three times a year. He claimed that he had made an international reputation by thinking as often as once a week! And please remember that there is no expedient to which a person will not resort to avoid the labor of thinking.

It will be more important now than ever before to shine up all the instruments in your kit that may prove to be the tools to success. We are coming out into a tough and tangled world. Those who are well-equipped will survive. Those who are not, may not. In almost every life, in every age, one gets what one asks for, and in this age of all others there will be very few alibis allowed.

There is not much of a secret to success. It is a great thing that is usually won by humble, routine methods. The mere decision you made to begin these lessons was an important step, for, as the Chinese say, "The journey of a thousand miles begins with a single step."

So continue with your word study. Watch for new words at all times. Never be content until you know the meaning of a strange one. Make it your own possession. Use it in a letter, in conversation. List it in your pocket notebook, with its common meaning, its pronunciation, and a sentence in which it is used. Have a little mental rehearsal on these words now and again while you are walking along the street. Carry on an imaginary conversation.

An intelligent argument, by the way, will give your new words a real workout. In such a challenge, a sharply accurate knowledge of the exact meanings of words is invaluable.

We can take particular and patriotic pride in mastering our speech. For ours is no longer the English language. It is the American language. Our language is as different from so-called English as South American Spanish is from the Castilian Spanish of Spain.

As a matter of fact, there is no true "English" language, as Scotland, Ireland, and Wales, and the various areas of England itself, all have their dialects. The Lincolnshire farmer and the Lancashire miner can't even understand each other. England, like almost every other nation in the world, is a mass of discordant dialects.

What we know as the "English" language is, much more truly, the "London" language, and the language of a particular part and class of London at that, as the inhabitants of Limehouse might laugh at the cockney dialect.

So there is every reason why you should take a deep and passionate pride in the American language. It has a beautiful unity throughout our land. No other country in the world one-tenth our size can show such linguistic solidarity, nor any approach to it. This American language is your creation; it belongs to you, and the more you master it, the more secure you will feel in every aspect of your personal, social, and professional or business life.

Index

Only the first appearance of each word in each chapter is indicated.

About the Authors

Dr. Wilfred Funk and Norman Lewis were both deeply concerned with the history and use of the English language for many years. As editors, lexicographers, teachers, and authors, they both contributed extensively to this important field. As collaborators in producing *30 Days to a More Powerful Vocabulary*, their success was even greater. In various editions, this book has sold nearly four million copies.

CPSIA information can be obtained
at www.ICGtesting.com
Printed in the USA
BVHW080844170223
658564BV00003B/3